LEGAL EAGLES

by Mr Phil Wilson
(LLB Hons) Solicitor

LEGAL EAGLES

by Mr Phil Wilson
(LLB Hons) Solicitor

xpl publishing

© xpl publishing and the Authors 2004

Published by
xpl law
31–33 Stonehills House
Welwyn Garden City
Hertfordshire
AL8 6PU

ISBN 1 85811 305 9

Typeset by Jane Conway

Cover design by Jane Conway

Printed in Great Britain by Lightning Source

CONTENTS

INTRODUCTION

P.E. WILSON is a solicitor who started his legal career as an office junior law clerk with a firm of City solicitors before moving on to a West End firm. After six years experience of clerking in the High Court, Divorce Registry, Bush House etc., he left to further his studies to qualify as a solicitor. He also has several years experience in crime and police station attendance prior to qualification as a solicitor.

P.E. WILSON is also the founder of Legal Lifesavers a trading name for Lifesaver Limited which is an Agency formed in 1994. The Agency provides a comprehensive recruitment, clerking services and paralegal support to the solicitor's profession by trained and experienced law clerks, as well as law graduates, including those seeking trainee contracts/pupillage and legal executives. The services are provided to solicitors in London and throughout the UK.

The Aims of the Book

This book is designed to help those persons interested in working in the legal field and have some or no legal qualifications or practical experience or training and wish to obtain an insight into the nature of the work carried out in a solicitors' practice including those upon which they may be called upon to perform.

This book not only aims to assist the student with the practical experience and functions of a paralegal but also to promote confidence so that the student can perform the task requested of him or her from the solicitors with confidence. Further this book can be used as a guide when the student begins his career as a full-time or freelance paralegal including trainee solicitors during the early part of their training.

Solicitors concerned to ensure their clerks are aware of the shifts required will find the guide invaluable.

The book is also designed to be used as a study guide during Legal Lifesavers (LLS) paralegal/court clerking courses and contains fictional cases studies to be used as a guide in order for the trainee paralegal to relate to what is expected of them as a qualified paralegal and can also be used as a reference when practising as a paralegal.

Some Notes

Further, in this manual the masculine includes the feminine and the singular the plural where the context admits and where there are two or more persons included in the expression Clerk, paralegal, Counsel or Solicitors.

I would also like to dedicate this book to my wife Deirdre for her help and support throughout the creation of Legal Lifesavers and the writing of this book.

I would like to also thank Barbara Robinson for her assistance with the typing.

Finally, at the time of going to press the information contained in this book had been researched as correct and I therefore cannot accept responsibility for any changes. Although the contents will be periodically reviewed should any reader come across any amendments prior to such review then do please write to us, c/o the publishers.

CHAPTER 1
WHAT IS CLERKING?

Defining Clerking

In order to appreciate the importance of the role of the clerk and what clerking entails, it is necessary to discuss and look briefly at how a trainee solicitor becomes a qualified solicitor and at the solicitor's practice itself.

Firstly it should be noted that every solicitor has done some form of clerking at some stage in his or her legal career. This might be in the form of attending on a trial/hearing or conference with counsel or simply attending court to issue a document. In order for trainee solicitors to qualify as solicitors, they have to be trained by a more senior solicitor known as their principal. This final stage of the trainee solicitor's training could be described as an apprenticeship.

At this stage of the trainee solicitor's career in addition to interviewing, advising and taking action on behalf of clients under the watchful eye of their principal, part of their training will involve some element of clerking. This element of clerking could be described as the **foundation or cornerstone** of clerking in the individual solicitor's career, as once qualified this type of clerking will be diminished. This is also important, for the solicitor who intend to practice on their own later on in their career. Clerking properly is therefore an important skill.

However, as the solicitor's time is more valuable in the office (including the trainee solicitor), it is more economical to train or allocate the full-time element of this clerking role to members of staff now commonly known as Outdoor Clerks/Law Clerks often known as Paralegals.

You can see that paralegals have a very important role to play in the legal profession. The paralegal's duties are wide and varied, ranging from having their own case-load under supervision, attending trials/hearings with counsel, conferences, applications before District Judges or High Court Masters, to filing/issuing documents at court.

Clerking could therefore be described as the **Delegated Legal and Court Administration work of a solicitors' practice**:

- Delegated

   This means any area of work that a solicitor can safely pass to paralegal staff to carry out under supervision.

- Legal

   This simply means the legal aspect of the matter: for example, the requirement of the solicitor to attend court with a barrister or arrange for a representative to attend on his behalf. This would include dealing with own case-load under supervision.

- Court Administration Work

   This involves the preparation and administration work involved in a matter including bringing the matter to court. This would include the issuing or filing of a document at court or other administrative procedural work such as: entering judgment; filing an acknowledgment of service form or carrying out searches. In short, the presentation of the papers to be entered on, the court record and/or making enquiries with regards to a particular case.

What is a Paralegal?

A paralegal can therefore be described as the person who carries out the delegated legal and court administrative work of a solicitors' practice.

Qualifications

In order to be taken on by a solicitors' practice with a view to being trained as a paralegal, most firms would request that you have a minimum of at least four GCSE's or O levels. However if you are already fully trained or have experience of benefit to the firm, in most cases this will be more important than qualifications, especially if you have plenty of common sense. In any event most solicitors normally encourage their staff to further their education with a view to obtaining a qualification.

Therefore it can be seen that although qualifications are important, experience and common sense are more important to the average firm.

Who does Clerking?

The type of people who do clerking varies. They range from the 16 year old office junior to the retired pensioner who is still very active. People do clerking for different kinds of reasons. You have the 16 year old who is just starting out in his legal career and you have those in the middle who have for a number of years done clerking as their full-time job. At the other end you have the active pensioner who does clerking to supplement his pension – for example the retired policeman. You also have the freelance clerk who is looking a full-time job but does clerking in the interim for example those who have finished either their law degree, Bar or law school and wish to gain legal experience and make contacts which might help them later on in their career.

From this you will see the type of people who do clerking varies considerably and each have their own particular reason for doing it.

Clerks are important not only because it is cheaper to send a clerk to court instead of a solicitor or another fee earner whose time is more valuable in the office working on the files but also it makes economic sense to have someone or use someone whose job is to specialise in doing the clerking.

Who uses Clerks?

Almost every solicitors' practice uses a clerk for one reason or another. The larger firms tend to employ full-time clerks whilst the smaller firms have lists of clerks, which they use from time to time on a freelance basis.

Duties of Paralegal Clerks

The major work of a clerk entails attending courts with counsel. This might be at the Crown Court, County Court, the High Court of Justice (otherwise known as the Royal Courts of Justice) or the Principal Family Registry at First Avenue House. Occasionally the clerk may be requested to attend a Tribunal hearing.

Other duties include issuing and filing documents or sometimes attending before the district judge in the County Court or High Court Masters in the Royal Courts of Justice or Principal Family Registry on a directions hearing.

If the clerk has been requested to attend court with counsel he should bear in mind that all the preparation should have been completed by the instructing solicitors and the clerk's main function at court is to be of maximum assistance to counsel (the barrister) and to look after the client when counsel is negotiating with the other party's barrister or legal representative.

The clerk's duties also include liaising with the office and keeping accurate records of the proceedings including:

*   keeping an accurate record of the times to and from court,
*   times waiting,
*   times in conference, and
*   times of the trial/hearing.

In certain cases the duties also include facilitating the passing of instructions from client to counsel and counsel to client.

Timekeeping

As a clerk you should pay a lot of attention to your timekeeping. You should aim to be at court at least 30 minutes before the hearing. You must remember that at court you are the face or representative of the instructing solicitor and everything that you do will reflect on the instructing solicitors' firm. If you are seeking regular work from the firm as a freelance clerk your timekeeping will also determine whether or not you are instructed in the future.

It is not only good professional practice to aim to arrive early at court, but it will also help you to keep calm and feel a part of the whole process from the beginning by being available to take part in the very first conference.

It is however appreciated that you may have been instructed at short notice or you may be late due to an "act of god" such as leaf on the British Rail line or some other unforseeable delay. However as a general rule you should aim to be at court at least 30 minutes beforehand. Where you have had the file overnight you should have no excuse.

CHAPTER 2
THE SOLICITORS FILE AND CONTENTS

Files are normally made up of documents and letters otherwise known as correspondence. Documents may be in the form of statements, proofs of evidence or affidavits. These documents, although under a different name, all contain clients' versions of events. There may also be statements from opposing parties giving their side of events.

An affidavit may refer to a document and this is normally referred to as an exhibit to the affidavit.

A file will also contain the brief or instructions to counsel (the barrister). The brief tells counsel what instructing solicitors require of him or her.

Although not an exhaustive list other documents in the file may be: an expert report; probation or welfare officer report or photographs. All of these depend on the particular case.

Receiving Files at Short Notice

In the event that clerks receive files at very short notice, it will be difficult to become fully conversant with the case. Instructing solicitors will be aware of this and in most cases counsel will be fully instructed.

In order for the clerk to know what the case is about it is recommended that he/she at least read the brief or instructions to counsel and the client's statement/proof of evidence or affidavits. If time is available the clerk should then browse through the correspondence (letters) just to familiarise him or herself with the various letters passing to and from the instructing solicitors.

The reason behind reading the correspondence is that counsel may be asked a question which he cannot answer. Counsel may then ask the clerk whether the instructing solicitors have for example, written to a particular person or body in order that counsel might explain or answer the question posed by the judge or the opposition counsel.

When the clerk receives the file in sufficient time, he or she should become as familiar as possible with the case and the various documents in the file in order to give maximum assistance to counsel.

In the event that you are given late instructions and you manage to find counsel and the client on your arrival, it is sensible to explain that you have only just been instructed and have not had time to familiarise yourself fully with the case. It may be better to ask counsel whether he/she wishes to browse through the correspondence file to see whether there is anything that he/she may need. This will be a lot quicker than you searching for a particular document in a file that you are not familiar with.

CHAPTER 3
THE LIST OFFICE

The list office is the department where the decision to list a case is made. The list officer is the person who decides which case is to be allocated to a particular courtroom.

Various courts have different names for this department, which are as follows:

- In the Magistrates' Court it is known as the Scheduling Office

- In the County Court and the Crown Court it is called the List Office

- In the High Court you should look for the Clerk of the List/Rules

All of these rooms perform the same function of allocating cases to the appropriate courtrooms.

Criminal Cases

If you are dealing with a criminal case listed as a floater, it may mean that you could be hanging around for the best part of the morning and afternoon waiting for a courtroom to become available.

The barrister and yourself may well be tannoyed now and again to go to the list office. This helps to keep everyone informed of what is happening including whether the matter is likely to be listed that day.

Some list offices can be quite helpful although others at times might seem unhelpful due to the stress placed on them by members of the profession and the nature of the job itself in trying to ensure that the list is cleared.

Under no circumstance should you leave the court if the matter is listed as a floater until you are told by the list office personally or over the tannoy system that you are released.

Civil Cases

In the other courts most of the cases are normally given a fixed date. This therefore alleviates the problem of attending court and waiting around for a court to become free.

However in the County Court unless the matter is listed for trial there will be some element of waiting. You can see from the above that although you may be given a particular time to attend the county court, other solicitors are given the same time. Upon arrival at court the usher will decide which case is to be heard first based on who is ready at that particular time.

CHAPTER 4
ON ARRIVAL AT COURT

On arrival at court the first job of the clerk is to find out the number of the court in which the case will be heard. This will involve checking the court list which is normally pinned to the notice board or wall in the reception area. Sometimes the security personnel at the door have a list and may be able to assist you.

The list should always be checked even if the instructing solicitors have already been given a courtroom number. The reason for this is that sometimes the list office may change the number of the courtroom at short notice.

Once you have found the list you should record the following:

- the court
- the courtroom number
- the name of the judge
- the name of counsel
- the name of the instructing solicitors for the other side

If you are a freelance clerk working for different firms you should also record the name of the solicitors currently instructing you. The reason for this is that if you are instructed by other firms immediately after each case without having time to write up your attendance notes, this will avoid you getting the cases mixed up and sending the attendance notes to the wrong firm. It is therefore recommended that as a matter of course, the name of the instructing solicitors should be recorded.

You should remember to pay attention to your timekeeping (see, Chapter 1 above). It can be rather embarrassing arriving late when counsel is in conference and you have to interupt his chain of thought to introduce yourself both to him and the client. It is also a good idea to be early to meet the client. If this is their first time in court they may well be wandering around looking lost.

Finding Counsel and Client

If the client and counsel are not known to you by sight, check if there is a tannoy system in the court. If so, you should put a tannoy out for counsel and client to meet you at the reception area in the vicinity of that particular court. In the meantime it may be necessary to ask around and suffer the embarrassment of approaching anyone who would fit the description of the client. If you do see someone do not be afraid to approach him or her and ask them if they are "Mr or Mrs Bloggs" as the case may be.

If it is a criminal matter you should check the file for a custody record which will have the description of the client including his height, weight, date of birth, colour etc. You should also check the correspondence to see whether or not the client is in custody by looking for letters addressed to him to see whether they were sent to a prison or a residential address.

If the client is in custody then it is pointless tannoying for him as he will be produced directly in court and it is highly likely that counsel might be in the cells with him. It is therefore wise to check with the cells to see whether counsel is having a conference with the client.

In visiting the cells be prepared to be searched and to hand over your mobile phone until the conference is over.

If you have tried all of the above without success, then you should report to the usher and check whether counsel had already reported in.

Counsel could be in any room having a conference. In such case you could either check the conference rooms and face the embarrassment of being given some stern looks or abrupt answers or simply wait outside the courtroom.

If the client has not arrived at court and the hearing time is drawing close you should check the file for a telephone number and check to see whether the client has left. You should also telephone the instructing solicitors to find out whether the client has contacted them to say he is experiencing some problems getting to court. You should also check the file to see if there is a letter informing him of the court hearing so this letter can be shown to the judge in the event that the client does not turn up. If the client has telephoned the office this will enable the barrister to explain the client's absence to the judge and it demonstrates that you have done everything you can to locate the client.

In the event the client does not turn up, the judge in a criminal case may issue a warrant for his arrest. This warrant may be backed for bail in certain circumstances. In a civil or family matter the client may have a judgment or decision made against him.

Once you have found the client you should introduce yourself by saying, "I am Mr Bloggs of Very Good Solicitors. I will be assisting the barrister in your case".

Counsel not at Court

In the event that you cannot find counsel you should carry out the standard procedures outlined above. You must remember that counsel will be looking for you and you should listen out for a tannoy requesting the representative from your instructing solicitors firm or the representative in the case of your client, to report to the reception area.

Barristers have there own robing rooms where they change into their wigs and gowns. You can always enquire there if necessary. Most solicitors' firms normally use a particular barristers' chambers and if you are instructed regularly by that firm, you will also become familiar with most of the barristers from that chamber.

If time is drawing close, you should check if there is a number on file for counsel's chambers and if so telephone to find out whether counsel has left. It is not unknown for instructing solicitors to forget to remind counsel's clerk of an adjourned hearing.

You should telephone the office to enquire whether counsel has been instructed only as a last resort, to avoid getting counsel into trouble with your instructing solicitors.

If there are only 15 minutes left before the hearing and counsel has still not arrived then you should telephone the office. In any event it is imperative that you keep the usher informed of the progress you have made. You should also be prepared as the instructing solicitors representative to explain to the judge what has happened.

Relieving someone or arriving late at Court

In the event that you are given late instructions or instructed to relieve someone already at court and the court is in progress, you should check the list for the courtroom number and the name of the judge as outlined above.

On arrival outside the courtroom you should not knock but simply open the courtroom door quietly and upon entering bow to His Honour the judge and then go and sit behind your counsel.

If upon your arrival counsel is on his feet and in full flow making representations/submissions do not disturb him but simply sit behind him until he has finished. Even then it might be wise to write him a note pointing out that you have arrived to assist him rather than attempting to speak to him direct.

Etiquette of the Court

Whenever you enter or leave a court, providing the judge is sitting, always bow to the judge. Whenever the judge enters or leaves the courtroom everyone will be asked to stand.

Always wear dark clothing and avoid bright colours or dressing as though you are going to the local disco. Men should always wear a suit and tie. Also remember to switch off your mobile phone to avoid a public rebuke by the judge.

CHAPTER 5
TAKING NOTES

Where you are attending on a trial in addition to the information to be recorded from the list you should record the time you arrived at court. You should attempt to make your notes as good and legible as possible. You should record whether it is day 1 or 2 of the trial and always record the name of the witness that is being called, including the time that they were called.

It is appreciated that in trying to keep up even the notes of those with the best handwriting can sometime become illegible and can only be read by that person. However by taking good notes from the outset it will save you a lot of work at the end of the trial. This will be explained in Chapters 6 and 7. Your notes may also be required in relation to an appeal.

The style of taking notes at court is down to personal choice. They are normally taken in one of the two following forms:

* notes of questions and answers
* notes of answers only

(i) Notes of the Questions and Answers

If you feel comfortable and are able to write quickly enough to keep up and make notes of the questions and answers given throughout the trial, then this is the style for you. However you have to be able to concentrate because with this style you may sometimes find that by the time you have finished writing down the questions posed you may have forgotten what the answers were.

This style is very helpful to the instructing solicitors in the event that there is an appeal but unless you are very quick to get the information

down there is always a possibility that you may miss some of the
questions and answers.

(ii) Notes of Answers only

With this style of note taking you can keep a more accurate record of
what the witnesses said in giving evidence and notes can be taken at
a more reasonable pace.

With this style you simply record the answers given by the witness.
More importantly the questions can normally be deciphered from the
answers given by the witness.

However difficulty may arise where the witness simply answers "yes"
or "no". In such cases you should record "no" followed by the question
– for example "No I did not steal the car" or "Yes I own a blue car" etc.
Even the judge and barrister only make notes of the answers given
although the examining barrister will have notes of the questions.

Which Style should you Adopt?

Out of the two styles it is recommended that you adopt the second
option of noting the answers only, unless you are confident you can
keep up and make full notes of the questions and answers posed
throughout the trial.

You should however be able to adapt your notetaking depending on
whom is speaking. It is recommended that you adopt a hybrid or
combination of the two styles of taking notes above namely,
recording the answers given by the witnesses as in (ii) adopting (i) by
recording both the questions and answers given when the judge
interrupts or intervenes and poses a question.

Why are your Notes Important?

Although a transcript of the trial will be available your notes are
normally required by the instructing solicitors in the event that there
is an appeal. This is one of the reasons why it is important to make
your notes as legible as possible.

One of the most important parts of the trial where it is imperative that you take good notes is when your barrister is cross-examining a prosecution or opponent's witness. You must remember that whilst counsel is on his/her feet asking questions of a witness they cannot take good notes and some barristers will rely on their solicitors' representative to make reliable notes. At the end of the hearing the barrister may take your notes away to read overnight.

If you have to attend a witness during the proceedings, this will obviously mean that you can not continue to take notes. The same applies where you have to attend the client in the dock at the back of the court to take instructions or carry out some task requested by counsel. In such case you should write in your notes "attending client or witness" as the case may be. This will explain any gaps in your notes.

CHAPTER 6
HOW TO DO ATTENDANCE NOTES

In most cases the average freelance clerk when writing their attendance notes normally concentrates primarily on what happened in the courtroom. They seldom write about the conference that took place before entering or leaving the courtroom.

Attendance notes should therefore be in three parts and should contain details of what happened:

- before the hearing
- during the hearing
- after the hearing

This is particularly important during interlocutory hearings which are matters listed not as trial but perhaps for between 10 minutes and an hour for directions.

If your attendance notes contain the above three elements then you will have a satisfactory attendance note to take to your instructing solicitors.

You should always bear in mind that the more detailed your attendance notes are, the more firms may request your services and be pleased that you are covering their cases.

If you are looking for a training contract or a full-time position it could mean the difference between getting the position and continuing to clerk.

What should your Attendance Note contain?

You should put yourselves in the instructing solicitors' position in which case you would want to know as much as possible of the whole day in court. This does not mean you should write down everything verbatim about what was said prior to the hearing. You will have to use your own discretion and common sense and only make notes of what you feel is relevant.

The attendance notes should contain details of *all* your time spent travelling to and from court and the time spent at court together with the details you should have recorded from the list such as the name of the judge court, counsel, and courtroom number etc.

Your full name should be recorded at the top of your attendance note (see specimen). The first paragraph should start with your initials such as "PW" and the name of the court and the type of the hearing you have attended. Therefore an attendance note should commence "PW attending Bromley County Court on directions hearing".

This automatically reminds the instructing solicitors which court the matter was listed in and what the case was about.

It is also sensible to record what happened on your arrival at court, such as whether counsel or the client was present, including any other parties such as an interpreter. You should then record whether or not you went into conference and what was discussed followed by notes of what happened during and after the hearing. You should record details of the times spent in conference, time spent waiting, travelling time and any out of pocket expenses incurred. If you are a car driver you should record details of your mileage.

When you attend interlocutory Directions hearings which are listed for 10 minutes to an hour, your notes can be re-written as the record will not be as long as for a full-blown trial. Therefore although it is always advisable to take legible notes from the outset providing you can read the notes to re-write them in a legible form this will be acceptable.

Should you Re-Write your Notes?

Where you have attended on a trial however you will not be able to re-write all your notes. In this case all you would need to do is give a brief summary in your attendance note of what happened and if it is the last day of the trial always write out the decision, judgment or verdict. At the bottom of your attendance note you can refer the instructing solicitors to your trial notes for further details. Making the trial notes as clear as possible will mean that you will not have to re-write them but simply refer the reader to them.

Recording your Time

You should bear in mind the metre does not start to run to record your time until you have picked up the file from the instructing solicitors. It will stop running upon you returning the file to the firm the same day or if you take the file away overnight, upon your arrival home. If you have a file in your possession prior to attending court, the metre will start running from the minute you leave home.

It is important to accurately record your time as this will enable the instructing solicitors to make up an accurate bill.

CHAPTER 7
COURTROOM OFFICIALS

The standard officials in the Crown Court are as follows:

- the Judge
- the Clerk
- the Stenographer
- the Usher

Other parties in the court are:

- the Jury
- Barristers
- Solicitors and Crown Prosecution/Opponent's representative
- Client/Defendant
- Prison Officer

Civil or Family Court proceedings do not normally involve the jury and prison officer. The defendant or respondent does not sit in the dock but instead sits next to his solicitors.

The Judge

The judge sits on a raised platform in the courtroom and is normally facing the defendant who sits in the dock at the back of the court. The judge sits in a position where he has full view of the courtroom and other officials. Unless or until the defendant is found guilty the judge's role is more like a referee to ensure fair play. The judge decides on the law but it is the jury who decides whether the defendant is guilty or not.

Where the jury finds the defendant guilty, the judge in sentencing the defendant to a term of imprisonment, normally gives a short speech such as "You are a menace to society and it is my duty to protect the public and send a signal to others etc.". In short the judge normally "throws the book" at the defendant before sending him to prison. If the judge is considering an alternative sentence he will still give a speech before telling the defendant that he is giving him a second chance.

The Court Clerk

Sitting below the judge is the clerk whose duties include swearing in the juries, reading or putting the charges to the defendant and generally assisting with the smooth-running of the trial.

The Stenographer/Shorthand Typist

The stenographer is the shorthand typist whose job is solely to record the proceedings. This includes evidence given by the witnesses, submissions and representations made by the barristers and the judge's rulings and summing up. In short the stenographer records whatever is said in relation to the trial at court.

From this record, a transcript of the proceedings can be obtained if necessary. Where no stenographer is in court, the proceedings are tape-recorded by the clerk.

The Usher

Sitting to the side or in front of the clerk is the court usher whose function is to open the court, call the witnesses into court and pass documents from the barristers to the judge. The usher also asks everyone to stand when the judge enters and leave the courtroom.

The usher acts as the jury bailiff who is normally sworn in after the judge has summed up. Other duties include assisting in the smooth-running of the trial.

The Jury

The jury are twelve ordinary men and women from different backgrounds called at random to sit as members of the jury known as "jury service".

The jury normally sits at the side closest to the defence in a position where they have a good view of the whole courtroom. They are positioned so they can see the judge, the defendant, the witnesses and the barristers.

At trial although some barristers will explain to the client the purpose and function of the jury you should also explain to the client/defendant that he can challenge any members of the jury to prevent them from being sworn in, providing he/she has good reason. The client cannot object simply because he does not like the way the potential juror looks or dresses. An acceptable reason might be where the jury member might be known to the defendant client in which case the barrister should be told. Any challenge must be made before the oath is taken by the potential juror.

Although you may in some cases bump into members of the jury outside the courtroom under no circumstances should you speak to any of them. This also applies to the barristers themselves.

At the end of the hearing a jury bailiff will be sworn to look after the jury and ensure that no one speaks to them. The bailiff will take an oath saying amongst other things "I will not speak to them myself, or suffer anyone to speak to them unless it be to ask if they be agreed upon their verdict".

Whenever the oath is being taken by the jury under no circumstances should you attempt to speak or leave the courtroom. If so it may result in you being rebuked by the court clerk.

The Defendant

The defendant normally sits at the back of the court in the dock with a prison guard. The dock is on a raised platform so that the defendant like the judge can see what is going on throughout the trial. In civil matters the client will sit next to his solicitors or representative.

CHAPTER 8
PROCEDURE IN COURT

In court the barristers sits in the front row or bench facing the judge. The clerks and solicitors sit in the row behind.

The general rule regarding court procedure is that the prosecution, plaintiff or party bringing the application will address the court first, once the judge takes his seat and the hearing commences.

When the hearing commences in most cases the defendant's bail position will be discussed and the judge may confirm or vary the clients bail conditions for the duration of the trial. The defendant is normally told not to leave the court building.

Once this has been addressed the accused will be arraigned. This simply means that the indictment which contains details of the charges against him will be read or put to him and he will either plead guilty or not guilty.

The jury will then be sworn in and after any excess jury members leave the courtroom counsel for the prosecution will make an opening speech giving details of the case against the accused client, which is brought by the Crown.

At this point anyone sitting in the courtroom might feel that the accused is guilty and does not stand a chance but this will be balanced out later when the defence presents its case.

The prosecution witness will then be called and examined by the prosecution barrister. You should be able to follow what the witnesses are saying from the bundle of statements (normally called the committal bundle), which you should have on file. In any event you should be making notes by now of what the witnesses are saying.

The prosecution witnesses will then be cross-examined by the defence counsel to try and discredit their evidence. Where the defence counsel has exposed holes in the prosecution case, the prosecution will then be given the opportunity to re-examine the witness to try and repair any damage done as a result of the defence counsel's cross-examination.

It is at this point in time when your barrister is cross-examining or putting questions to the prosecution witness, that you should be taking reliable and detailed notes of either the questions and answers or simply the answers given by the witness.

After re-examination the judge may sometimes have some questions to put to the witness.

Once the prosecution has called their last witness their case will end.

Counsel for the prosecution will have acknowledged at the beginning in the opening speech that it was for the prosecution to prove their case beyond a reasonable doubt.

If the prosecution has failed to prove that there is a prima facie case against the defendant, then once the prosecution case has closed, the defence may make a submission, in the absence of the jury, that there was no case to answer or that it would be unsafe and unsatisfactory to leave the case to the jury.

If the defence are successful in their representations and submissions the case will come to an end.

If no representations are made or the submissions are rejected by the judge then the defence will present their case and call their first witness which is normally the defendant, followed by any other witnesses.

At the conclusion of the defence case the prosecution barrister will make a speech to try and persuade the jury that they should find the defendant guilty. The defence counsel will make a final speech and request that the jury find the defendant not guilty.

Summing Up

The judge will then sum up the hearing. At this point in the trial the court usher will have put a sign on the outside of the courtroom door saying, "Quiet please judge summing up".

The summing up is very important and detailed notes should be made because if the judge misses certain points it can give rise to an appeal.

The judge must remind the jury of the burden of proof, that this burden rests on the prosecution and that the jury should be satisfied of the defendant's guilt. The judge will remind the jury that it was not for the defence to prove anything in the case.

The judge will tell the jury that they must consider the case based solely on the evidence presented by the Crown and the defence. He will elaborate on the evidence given by the witnesses and remind them that it is for them to decide. He will say that if they are not satisfied of the defendant's guilt so as to be sure of it then they should find the defendant not guilty.

The judge will also go through the charges on the indictment explaining what the jury need to find. This will include the law relating to the offence and the various elements the jury need to have found to have been met before they can convict the defendant.

The judge will give his opinion and point out any inconsistencies and contradictions in the evidence. He will explain to the jury that if they do not agree with him, they should ignore his opinion on the particular piece of evidence when considering their verdict.

Once the judge has finished summing up the jury bailiff will be sworn in and the jury will be asked to elect a member as foreman. They will then be asked to retire to reach a verdict.

The judge will remind them that they should ignore anything they may have heard with regards to a majority verdict and should try to reach a unanimous verdict. If when the time comes they still cannot reach a verdict then the judge will address this point again.

The jury will then retire to the jury room to deliberate. You should make a note of the time at which they do this.

In a civil or family matter the judge will not sum up but will retire to consider the judgment once both the plaintiff's and defendant's barristers have completed their closing speech.

The Verdict

When the jury has reached a verdict or, in a civil or family matter, when the judge has considered the judgment, the parties will be called back to the court. In a criminal case the foreman will be asked by the clerk whether they have reached a verdict to which they all agree. The foreman will then proceed to say whether they have found the defendant guilty or not guilty.

In a civil or family matter the judge will give an explanation as to why the decision was given in favour of the particular party.

If the defendant has been found guilty in a criminal trial the judge will either adjourn the hearing for pre-sentence reports to be prepared or may proceed to sentence the defendant.

The prosecution will then read out the defendant's previous convictions (if any) and details of the defendant's income with regards to costs and a fine.

If the judge decides to proceed to sentencing the defence barrister will then proceed to mitigate on behalf of the defendant to try and get the minimum sentence possible or avoid a custodial sentence at all.

CHAPTER 9
DEALING WITH THE CLIENT

Client giving Evidence

The client should be told of the procedure for giving evidence. It should be explained that he or she will have to take the oath which involves swearing on the bible or other holy book depending on the client's faith "to tell the truth and nothing but the truth". The client will be asked to affirm the above if he/she has no religion.

The client should be reminded that although the barristers will be speaking to him or her, the answers should be directed at the jury. The client should also be told to speak up so that the jury can hear what is said clearly. In addition the judge and other representatives including barristers, will be making a note of what is being said by the witness.

The client should be advised to answer "yes" or "no" to questions or to reply "don't know" or "cannot remember" as the case may be, unless the question calls for a more detailed answer.

Before going into court it may be wise to give the client a copy of his/her statement to refresh his/her memory. The client should be told that once he/she has been sworn in to give evidence neither the barrister nor yourself can discuss the case with the client any further until he or she has finished giving evidence. This does not mean you cannot talk to the client generally explaining court procedure or what will happen next. It simply means that you or the barrister cannot discuss the case with the client.

If the person giving evidence is an independent witness the barrister will not be able to speak to that witness at all. It will therefore be left to you, as the solicitors representative to inform him or her when they will be required and explain the procedure for giving evidence, as outlined above. Once the witness has been sworn in the same procedure applies in that neither the barrister nor yourself can speak to him or her about the case.

In circumstances where there is more than one witness, do not allow one to speak to another who is still giving evidence under oath where the matter has been adjourned.

Some clients might be unsure as to how to behave, what to do with their hands when they are in the witness box or how to address anyone in the courtroom.

The client or witness should be told to avoid folding their arms as it could be interpreted as disrespectful and intimidating to the jurors or even the judge. The client should either hold onto a rail if there is one or keep his or her hands at their sides, in front or behind.

The client should address the judge as "Your Honour" or simply answers the questions without referring to the title of the court personnel.

Taking Instructions from the Client

In a civil matter the client will be sitting next to you and you can therefore take instructions there and then and pass the information to counsel who will be sitting in front. In some cases the client will speak directly to counsel. If counsel is on his feet and is in full flow addressing the court it is advisable not to interrupt him but simply make a note of the client's instructions and put it on the desk in front of him.

In a criminal trial the client will not be sitting next to you but instead will be sitting in the dock (in most cases directly behind you).

A problem will arise where the client wishes to pass a message to counsel. As you will have your back to the client, short of him or her calling, you will not know when to attend and take instructions.

It is therefore advisable to point out this problem to the client beforehand and to leave a pen and some paper cut into squares with the client so that he or she can write out whatever note or message he or she wishes to pass to counsel. The client should also be told to clear his or her throat to prompt you to turn around or to attract the attention of the court usher who will ask you to attend and see him or her.

If this happens simply get up and approach the client and take the client's instructions. There is no need to bow to the judge, as you are not leaving the courtroom. Don't forget to take your writing pad with you. Once you have attended the client you can speak to him or her quietly, making a note if he or she has not already done so to give to counsel on your return to sit down.

Sometimes the client may simply want to attend to a "call of nature" in which case the hearing will need to be adjourned.

Where a client is constantly making notes to pass to counsel you should screen them to ensure that the client is not referring to something which counsel has already addressed. In any event it is advisable to inform the client that he or she should not attempt to pass notes to counsel on everything which he disagrees with. Counsel should already be aware of these issues from reading his proof of evidence or statements. The client should only pass notes with regards to new issues which have been mentioned in court.

Advising the Client

Under no circumstances should you advise the client – that is counsel's job. Sometimes the client may ask you a question and you may be tempted to advise him. *Resist this temptation* and explain that counsel is the person who should answer the question. Explain that you will put the question to counsel when he or she returns.

In the event that you do advise the client, you may end up being embarrassed and create an atmosphere between yourself and counsel. The client may complain if the result is contrary to your advice and you may end up being rebuked by your instructing solicitors.

If in doubt as to how to handle the situation you can always explain that counsel is the best person to ask since he/she may have information from the other side of which you are not aware and therfore counsel's advice may be different to what you would give.

Client unhappy with Counsel

In the event that client express to you in confidence his unhappiness with counsel, this should be dealt with caution. It might be the first time that the client has met this counsel or the client may not like the advice that he has been given because it is not favourable. This does not necessarily mean that counsel is incompetent but indicates the complete reverse in that counsel is pointing out all the pros and cons of the case. Counsel has to give the good as well as the bad news.

In such a case you should side with counsel and express your confidence in counsel particularly if you have worked with him or her in the past. You should bear in mind that you may be dealing with a difficult client who complains about anything and everything including the instructing solicitors.

Sometimes if you express your confidence in counsel privately this normally helps to put the client at ease.

You could ask the client to allow you to at least mention whatever his or her concern is to counsel who in most cases would endeavour to explain the position again to the client and the reasons behind it, in order to alleviate the client's fears or concerns.

After a hearing some clients irrespective of any reassurance, will state point-blank that they do not wish to have that barrister representing them in any other forthcoming hearing. In such cases simply make a note of the client's complaint or request and report back to the instructing solicitors.

Dealing with the Client's Friends

Although it is very comforting for the defendant to have friends and relatives attending court to give moral support, it can in some cases have an adverse effect on him or her. Firstly in a jury trial, if the friends and relatives are rowdy this may influence the jury members perception and opinion of the client by allowing their individual prejudices to have some bearing on the ultimate decision.

If the friends are in the public gallery interrupting the proceedings this can result in a rebuke from the judge, which again would affect the jury and judge's perception of the defendant.

If the client has plenty of friends in attendance, you should explain to the client that certain friends and/or relatives may be better off staying out of the court room.

Concerned relatives attending court may wish to sit in the courtroom. You should always check with counsel first whether it is appropriate for that person to sit in the courtroom. If so, point where they should sit. You should remind them to switch off any mobile phones to avoid being publicly rebuked by the judge.

The Guilty Verdict

If the client is found guilty his/her reaction will depend on the advice given to him/her by counsel. Counsel should have already advised of the possibility of being found guilty and explained the potential range of sentences available to the judge, including the possibility of a prison sentence.

Some clients will either break down after the verdict is announced or break down outside the court if released on bail pending the preparation of a pre-sentence report. Some will break down in the cells if remanded in custody.

In such circumstances there is not a great deal that a clerk can say to reassure the client and it is therefore advisable to leave all the talking to the barrister. In most cases the barrister will be experienced in dealing with this situation.

At this stage the barrister should if he/she has not already done so, be explaining the possible sentence the client might get and be taking further instructions with regards to mitigating on behalf of the client when he or she comes up for sentencing.

The barrister may well ask for character references including information as to whether there is a possibility of the client obtaining a job if he/she is unemployed. The aim of this is to avoid the client going to prison.

In most cases the client will have relatives waiting in the court who will be quite anxious about how the client is coping if he/she is being held in custody. You should therefore ask the client if there are any messages he/she wishes to be relayed to them.

If the client smokes he may have already asked you or counsel for a cigarette and may well request that you ask the relatives to obtain some cigarettes. Each court has its own rules about the passing of cigarettes and you are therefore advised to check with the prison officers whether or not cigarettes can be passed to the client.

Sentencing

If the client has been sentenced to a term of imprisonment again he will be taken to the cells and counsel will seek to have a final conference there with him. Leave all the talking to counsel unless you feel that you can contribute something of value to the conference without making the client feel any worse.

Counsel will discuss the possibility of appealing the sentence with the client and may tell you that he will do an advice and grounds of appeal if appropriate.

Counsel may well decide to take your notes to compare with his own to check on the judge's summing up and the general conduct of the case with a view to obtaining grounds for an appeal. Hence it is very important to take the best notes possible throughout the trial in particular when counsel is on his feet and when the judge is summing up.

Sometimes the police officer in the case may have the client's belongings at court – these may have been part of the exhibits or evidence in the case. Now that the case is over the officer may tell you that the client can collect his belongings or that you can collect them there and then by signing for them on behalf of the client.

If the client is sentenced to a term of imprisonment however it is advisable that you do not sign for the client's belongings as this will mean that you may end up having to take them back to the office with you. If the belongings are quite bulky then you may have problems in transporting and storing them. It is therefore wise to arrange for one of the client's relatives to attend the police station and collect the belongings on the client's behalf. If so, arrange for the client to sign a form of authority for his belongings to be released to his friends or relatives or for the authority to be sent direct from the prison.

CHAPTER 10
DEALING WITH WITNESSES

Discussing the Case

The barrister can introduce himself but cannot discuss the case with a witness who is going to give evidence of fact. The instructing solicitors should have prepared a witness statement beforehand, which would have been included in the barrister's brief. You should explain this to the witnesses beforehand not feel they are being snubbed by counsel. Counsel is however able to speak to a witness who is going to give character evidence only.

This does not however mean that you cannot speak to the witness, to explain when the witness will be required to attend court or to give general information. The only time you cannot speak to that witness is when the witness has been sworn in court to give evidence and the hearing is adjourned which means the witness will still be under oath. It does not mean you cannot talk to the witness generally but under no circumstances should you discuss the case with the witness. Some witnesses may ask how they have done so far in the case and you should resist the temptation to answer explaining that you cannot discuss the case until they have finished giving evidence.

The witnesses should be asked either to wait outside the courtroom or in a specific place such as the canteen so that you can find them when counsel is ready. In any event they should listen to the messages relayed on the tannoy system. Where the defence is presenting its case it is advisable to ask the witness to wait outside the courtroom.

Explaining Procedure

If the witness is giving evidence for the first time you should explain the following procedure. The witness will be sworn in by being asked to swear on the Bible or other holy book or to affirm to tell the whole truth and nothing but the truth. He or she will then be examined by your barrister and then be cross-examined by the other side's barrister (i.e. counsel for the prosecution or opponent). He or she may be re-examined by your barrister again to clarify any points raised by the opponent to repair any damage. The judge may then also ask the witness some questions.

If it is a jury trial, you should ask the witness to direct his or her answers to the jury and speak loud enough for the court to hear.

It might be helpful to draw a diagram of the court showing the witness where the various court officials including the judge will be sitting. You should explain that if his or her throat is dry he or she can ask for some water. You should again remind the witness that once sworn in you cannot discuss the case any further.

After the hearing the judge will tell the witnesses that they are free to leave the courtroom or sit at the back to listen to the rest of the case.

It is only when the witness has been released that you can discuss the case with him or her. You can even comment on their performance.

Witness Expenses

When witnesses attend to give evidence of fact they are entitled to receive their out of pocket expenses. If a witness is giving character evidence only no expenses are payable.

The witness should be informed if they are entitled to their expenses. In the majority of cases where a friend or relative is attending as a witness they will normally refuse or are not concerned with their out of pocket expenses.

The out of pocket expenses take the form of travel fares and any loss of earnings. However the witness should be informed that there is a limit to the amount that the court will pay to any one witness.

In a criminal case the witness expense form can normally be obtained from the list or court office.

Taking a Witness Statement

Sometimes the instructing solicitors may have difficulty getting a witness to attend the office in order to take a statement. A witness may be discovered at the last minute and asked to attend court without a statement having been prepared.

If the witness is giving evidence of fact the barrister cannot discuss the case with the witness and you will be asked to take a statement for the barrister to give him or her a general idea of the evidence the witness is likely to give.

The witness statement should contain the following details:

• Name
• Address
• Date of Birth
• Occupation
• Professional Qualification
• Telephone number
• Details of the evidence

The details of the evidence will consist of the information the witness is likely to give. You should start off by stating whether or not the witness knows the defendant and if so, for how long or if the witness is related to the defendant in any way.

The second paragraph should then address the evidence that the witness will give. To ensure that you get all the relevant information down and to allow you to expand on what the witness is saying you should bear the following elements in mind when deciding to ask the witness a question namely:

• who?
• what?
• where?
• when?
• how?

- date
- time

If in doubt as to how to start the statement or its general layout *"don't panic!"*. If you have access to the file there should be a copy of the client's witness statement on it, which can be used as a guide. If not, simply follow the above procedure and you should be OK.

Once you have finished the statement you should read it back to the witness, make any necessary amendments and ask the witness to sign and date the statement. You should then hand the statement to counsel and if possible keep a copy for the file.

CHAPTER 11
AT THE END OF THE HEARING

On the conclusion of a court hearing you should ensure that you make contact with the instructing solicitors in the following ways

Reporting back to Instructing Solicitors

At the end of every hearing you should report back to the instructing solicitors by telephoning and informing them of the outcome. Sometimes counsel may say they will telephone the solicitors and inform them of the decision. Under no circumstances should you leave this to counsel. The instructing solicitors instructed both yourself and counsel separately and expect to hear from you. It is therefore your duty to report back to your instructing solicitors whether or not counsel has reported back. You will have complied with your duty even if the solicitor is unavailable and you have to leave a message with the receptionist, secretary or on the answering machine.

You will have seen the conduct of the hearing from a different perspective to counsel and some solicitors like to get a feedback on counsel's performance whom they might have instructed for the first time.

Case Summary

Once a case is over the file should be taken straight back to the instructing solicitors unless you are instructed otherwise or you anticipate that by the time you reach the firm they will be closed. If so you should take the file home and deliver it on the next available day.

You will not have time to organise and write up your attendance note in the proper form outlined in Chapter 6. You should therefore write what I call a "case summary".

This should provide the instructing solicitors with the bare details of what happened in court namely, the order made, the judgement, or the sentence imposed including any important or urgent information which the instructing solicitors should be made aware of or which needs to be brought to their attention immediately.

The case summary should be clearly headed as such and will consist of the following:

- date of attendance
- name of instructing solicitors
- name of client
- the court
- the courtroom number
- the judge
- name of counsel

A specimen case summary should read as follows:

"PW attending BROMLEY COUNTY COURT on a directions hearing when the following directions were given:"

You should then list the DIRECTIONS given or the ORDER made. At the end of the summary you should state "FULL DETAILED ATTENDANCE NOTE TO FOLLOW"

If there is any important information which the instructing solicitors need to know, you should make a note of this under a "PS" or "NB" and take the file straight back to the instructing solicitors attaching the case summary to the file.

CHAPTER 12
THE MAGISTRATES COURT

It should be noted that all criminal cases commence in the Magistrates' Court and depending on the seriousness of the case and representations made by the legal representatives, they are then transferred up to the Crown Court, which is the higher court.

You will seldom be asked to attend a Magistrates' Court. On the odd occasion you may be asked to attend to take notes of a witness who is giving evidence at a committal hearing. In such a case the defence is probing the prosecution case to enable it to make a submission that there was no case for their client to answer.

By taking notes of what the prosecution witness says the content can be referred to in the event that the matter goes to trial in the Crown Court and the witness gives contradictory evidence.

Another occasion when you might be asked to attend a Magistrates' Court is in a road accident case where the driver is being prosecuted. The solicitor may be representing the victim of the road traffic accident and will want to know whether the defendant driver was found or pleaded guilty to the offence in order to make a claim against the insurers.

There is no jury in the Magistrates' Court and like the judge in the County Court the magistrates and District Judge are judge and jury in one.

The magistrates consist of a lay bench, which is made up of three unqualified magistrates who are guided by a qualified clerk with regards to the law. Alternatively a single Judge known as a District Judge can sit alone and make a decision without the need for a clerk.

Before a magistrate or District Judge can decide whether to try a case there must be a mode of trial hearing. This is where the accused is invited to indicate his plea. In deciding whether they are able to hear the case the magistrates have to consider the seriousness of the offence and compare it with their sentencing powers.

The Magistrates' Court powers of sentencing are limited to six months custodial sentence per offence with an overall total of 12 months. Therefore if a defendant commits three offences which could technically carry six months custodial sentence each the maximum that the magistrates can sentence the defendant for is 12 months.

If the magistrates consider that the offence is so serious that a longer sentence is called for then they will decline jurisdiction. This means that they will decline to hear the case and the matter will be transferred to the Crown Court. The defendant will have no say in the matter in such a case. In any event certain offences can only be tried in the Crown Court.

A "summary" offence can only be heard in the Magistrates' Court. An "either way" offence can be heard in the Magistrates' or the Crown Court. Providing the magistrates' sentencing powers in relation to the offence permit them to hear the case they will give the defendant a choice as to whether he or she wishes the case to be heard in the Magistrates' Court or prefers to elect a Crown Court trial before a judge and jury.

If the defendant upon advice from his/her solicitor or barrister elects a Crown Court trial then the matter will be adjourned for a committal hearing. The magistrates deals with very minor offences and if you visit a Magistrates' Court you will notice that many defendants appear unrepresented because legal aid is not always available in the Magistrates' Court. In practice the solicitor normally attends court by himself unless a barrister has been instructed. Unlike the Crown Court there are no requirements for the barrister to be assisted by a clerk in this court. You would therefore be rarely called upon to attend a Magistrates' Court.

CHAPTER 13
THE CROWN COURT

The majority of your clerking may require you to attend trials at the Crown Court. The Crown Court normally has a jury who will decide whether or not the client is guilty, unless the hearing is an appeal from the Magistrates' Court, a bail application or the matter is listed for mention.

However if the matter is listed for a pleas and directions hearing, the judge, prosecution and defence carry out a form of stocktaking and review the whole case to check whether the parties have received all the documents requested. If not the judge will be asked to set a time for those documents to be served on each other. This hearing also gives the defendant an opportunity to plead guilty and get some credit for avoiding the cost of a full-blown trial.

If the client decides to plead guilty then the judge might sentence immediately but in most cases will adjourn for a pre-sentence report.

If the client pleads not guilty then the judge will hear representations from both the defence and prosecution barristers, make the necessary orders requested by both sides and then set a date when the matter will enter what is called the "warned list" period.

Warned List

The warned list is a period of time which ranges between one and two weeks where the parties are put on notice that the matter can be listed for trial at any time during the period.

This provides the instructing solicitors with a time limit in which to prepare the case.

Where the defence and prosecution have expert witnesses who need to attend and are experiencing difficulties with obtaining other witnesses the judge may fix a date for the trial, in which case the matter will be heard on that fixed date and not entered on the warned list.

Trials and Floater Trials

When the matter is entered on the warned list normally no courtroom is allocated during that period. You will have been told that the matter is listed as a "floater"

This simply means that no courtroom is currently available but that a trial is due to finish at any time which may mean that the barristers are making their closing speeches or the judge is summing up after which the jury will be sent out. Once this happens then that courtroom will become available.

Sometimes when the matter is listed as a floater you can end up sitting around waiting for most of the day before you are released to return on another day or the matter is entered on another warned list.

If the matter is called you will be told which courtroom to attend. In court counsel will sit on the front bench and you will sit in the next row behind. There might be a form already on the bench in front of you to complete, requesting the following information:

- the name of the person attending (yourself)

- solicitors' name and address

- the date

- the status of the person attending i.e. clerk, solicitor, outdoor clerk, legal executive, and whether you are engaged on another case.

This form should be completed and handed to the clerk of the court in order for the instructing solicitors to claim for your attendance.

Before the hearing commences you should be aware of the various witnesses involved in the case. Be ready to report to the barrister anything you think is suspicious, such as one witness speaking to another after giving evidence.

You might be rebuffed by the barrister but it is better to let him know and face the embarrassment of being put down.

You should generally be as helpful as possible to the barrister, which in turn will make his job easier.

CHAPTER 14
THE COUNTY COURT

There is no jury in the County Court. Instead a judge alone will make the final decision. The judge is therefore judge and jury in one.

The County Court deals primarily with family disputes such as divorce, injunctions, landlord and tenant matters and other civil disputes such as personal injury and debts.

If you are required to attend the County Court with a barrister the same procedure applies on arrival at court.

Once you have met the barrister, reported to the court and with all instructions having been taken from the client it is just a matter of waiting for your case to be called.

Although you may have been told a time for the hearing, it does not necessarily mean you will be heard at that time, unless the matter is listed for trial. There might be other cases listed at the same time and the court usher's decision on who to call will depend on which parties are ready.

Although a matter is listed for 10.30am, at 11.30am you might still be sitting and waiting to be called.

CHAPTER 15
THE ROYAL COURTS OF JUSTICE

The Royal Courts of Justice (RCJ) otherwise known as the High Court is based in The Strand, London WC2.

If you are required to attend a trial/hearing on arrival you may decide to check which courtroom you are listed in by finding the list in the main hall. This may however take some time since there are quite a number of courts in the building. In order to save time you should attend the Clerk of the List which is the office dealing with the listing of cases. Provide the official with the name of your client and the case number and he or she will tell you which court your matter is listed in.

You should have been given this information beforehand. Often however the courtroom number is changed at the last minute and you may well end up having to check with the Clerk of the List in any event to ascertain which court the matter is now listed in. Once you have found the courtroom the same principles and procedure apply with regards to assisting counsel.

Action Department

You may be required to attend and issue a particular document in the Queen's Bench or Chancery Division. For example, you may be asked to issue a writ, enter judgment or draw up an order. These are all done in the Action Department of the particular division.

If you are instructed to issue a document, which reads "In The Queen's Bench Division", you should simply ask the court officials for the Queen's Bench Action Department and you will be pointed in the right direction. Once you have reached that department, the particular room that you require will be clearly marked according to the initials of the plaintiff.

If you have to pay a fee there is a cashier room close by. If the matter is in the Chancery Division the fee can be paid in any of the cashier's rooms.

If you have never done this particular task before, explain this to the staff behind the counter and they will assist you as much as they can, including advising on the number of copies you will require.

In the event that you are short of copies there is a photocopying room, which is directly above the security guard at the entrance to the main hall.

If you have to issue or make enquiries in the Chancery Division the Action Department is situated in the Thomas Moore Building.

Judge in Chambers

You may be called upon to attend a bail application with the barrister before a judge in chambers. The judge in chambers is situated in the Bear Garden which is a meeting point where you can sit down and complete or sort out whatever work needs to be done before issuing a document or attending before the court.

Your instructing solicitors should have done the necessary preparation beforehand including the issuing of all the necessary documents. Your barrister should also have been fully instructed. Your job is therefore to attend as normal, make a note of the proceedings including the decision and be of full assistance to the barrister.

High Court Masters

High Court Masters are similar to District Judges in the County Court in that they deal with directions, hearings and day-to-day queries by the parties. In most cases you will need an appointment by issuing an application for directions.

In an emergency or when you simply need the authority of the High Court Master then you can attend before the Practice Master who is on duty to deal with daily queries. The High Court Masters take it in turn to sit as the daily Practice Master.

CHAPTER 16
THE PRINCIPAL REGISTRY OF THE FAMILY DIVISION

As its title denotes this is the principal court that deals with family disputes. You may be asked to attend a hearing in this court, which deals primarily with divorce, residence and contact applications in respect of children and other family disputes.

The Principal Registry of the Family Division was formerly situated at Somerset House, London WC2 but has been relocated and is now situated at First Avenue House 42–49 High Holborn London WC1V 6NP.

In this Division you can issue applications with regard to family matters, make enquiries about your particular case or attend trial or directions hearings.

On some occasions the case may be transferred over to the Royal Courts of Justice.

The Taxing Department of the Division is also situated at the same address.

If you are instructed to attend before the District Judge on a query or directions hearing, you may have to bespeak the file.

Bespeaking Files

This simply means requesting the court file. This is done by completing a standard file request form from the appropriate department indicating which room you wish the file to be taken to.

Once retrieved, a member of the court staff will take the file to the appropriate District Judge's room who will refer to it in order to decide whether or not to grant or deal with your request or query.

The standard file request form will require the following details:

- case number
- name of parties
- instructing solicitors
- opponent's solicitors
- District Judge's room number

Proceedings involving Children

The Children Act 1989 governs proceedings in relation to children.

In order to appreciate and follow this type of proceeding, the trainee paralegal should have a basic understanding of some of the provisions and principles of the Act.

The Non-Intervention Rule

The court will not make any order in respect of a child, unless it is satisfied that making the order is better for the child than no order at all.

The Concept of Parental Responsibility

This represents the rights, duties, powers, responsibilities and authority, which by law a parent has in relation to the child and his or her property.

(i) Parents of a child born during a marriage each have parental responsibility for that child.

(ii) More than one person may have parental responsibility and one will not lose parental responsibility merely because another acquired it.

(iii) Where more than one person has parental responsibility, each may act alone.

(iv) The unmarried mother of a child has parental responsibility for that child. The father can acquire parental responsibility by making an application to the court or by entering into a written agreement with the mother.

Section 8 Orders

The following orders are common in proceedings involving children:

(i) **the Residence Order** – this states with whom the child should live

(ii) **the Contact Orders** – this specifies with whom a child should stay or have contact

(iii) **the Specific Issue Order** – this order settles a specific dispute in relation to some specific aspect of the child's welfare/upbringing

(iv) **the Prohibited Steps Order** – this order prevents someone from following a course of action in respect of a child's upbringing without the consent of the court.

Who may apply for a Section 8 Order

The following persons qualify as of right:

(i) the parent or guardian
(ii) the person with a residence order in their favour

The following persons qualify to apply for **Contact** or **Residence Orders only**:

(i) the spouse or ex-spouse of a child of the family
(ii) anyone the child has lived with for at least three years
(iii) anyone with the consent of:

- each person with a residence order; or
- the local authority (if the child is in care); or
- each person having parental responsibility

Any other person for example, a grandparent, may apply to the court for leave to make an application.

CHAPTER 17
CONFERENCE WITH COUNSEL

A conference is a meeting between the barrister, solicitors and client to discuss the case.

In most cases the solicitor normally send a representative such as yourself to attend the conference.

The conference can either be at court, in the solicitors' office or in most cases at the barrister's chambers and normally takes at least an hour.

The conference in chambers is normally used to discuss the evidence and sort out any foreseeable problems before attending the trial. Action required after the conference may include obtaining further evidence or writing off for specific documents. A conference at court is primarily to take further instructions from the client before entering the courtroom as final preparation for the trial.

As the solicitors' representative all you will be required to do is to make a note of what was discussed in the conference together with any request by counsel to be reported back to the instructing solicitors.

You should remember to make a note of the total time spent in conference.

Clerks who have never attended on a conference are normally apprehensive because they feel it is quite a difficult task. You should rest assured however that the conference is no different from you discussing the case at court with the barrister. The only slight difference is the venue. The conference is normally held at the barrister's chambers or in some cases at the solicitor's office.

CHAPTER 18
WITHOUT NOTICE HEARINGS
(formerly EX PARTE HEARINGS)

If the hearing you are attending on is a without notice application this simply means that only you and your barrister will be attending as the other side or respondent have no notice of the hearing.

If it is a without notice application for an injunction you should be aware that you will be required to issue the application (see below). This is done by attending the court office with the client who should have made an affidavit prepared by the instructing solicitors. This affidavit might be unsworn and this will therefore need to be sworn.

CHAPTER 19
ISSUING A DOCUMENT

Issuing is done at the court office by presenting the document over the counter with the appropriate copies and fee. The document will be processed and entered in the court record and then stamped/sealed by the clerk. Unless instructed otherwise you will need to wait and collect the sealed document for the file or for service. Depending on the application the document received may contain the hearing date.

As a general rule you should always check to ensure that the documents have the necessary court stamp/seal and that the court date is entered. If this has not been done refer back to the clerk to correct it. If unsure check with the clerk who may be able to explain why the date stamp or seal was not entered.

If the client has to swear an affidavit sometimes the court may stamp the front. The most important part however is the attestation clause, which the court officer should complete and sign next to the client's signature. Some courts will also put the court seal on the document.

Your instructions may be to arrange for the client to swear the affidavit and then issue the application. In such a case, on arrival at court you should give the client the affidavit to read and any amendments made should be initialled. You should then attend the court office where an authorised court officer will deal with the swearing of the affidavit. This will involve the client swearing on oath or affirming that the contents of the affidavit are true. The client will be asked to sign the affidavit near the attestation clause at the bottom of the affidavit and to initial any amendments if not done so already.

Once the affidavit is sworn it should be taken to the court office, which is normally the same room in which the affidavit injunction application (with relevant copies and fee (where appropriate)) are handed over the counter to be issued.

The court staff will then indicate which judge and court will hear the application.

As this will be an without notice (ex parte) application it will be pointless checking on the list in the reception area. This matter will not have been listed since the court would only have been notified of its existence upon you attending and presenting the application.

Once the court clerk has told you which court to attend you should inform the barrister and wait outside that courtroom or listen for the matter to be called over the tannoy system.

CHAPTER 20
THE INJUNCTION ORDER

Where the injunction is granted the order will not be prepared straight away. This will therefore mean you waiting around at court for the injunction order which should be taken back to the instructing solicitors to be served on the respondent. Some courts have a policy where the injunction will not be ready until 3pm in the afternoon whereas others will prepare it within an hour or so.

You should therefore check with the court when the injunction order will be ready for collection in order to have an idea how long you are likely to wait.

Unless you are told otherwise you should report back to the instructing solicitors and ask them whether they want you to continue to wait.

Once the order has been collected, you should return it as soon as possible to the instructing solicitors.

Some firms my arrange for the process server to attend court and collect the documents, and serve them on the respondent at the same time.

CHAPTER 21
FILING/LODGING A DOCUMENT

As part of your instructions you may be asked to file or lodge a document at court. If it is in relation to the trial that you are attending on you should give the document to counsel, the court usher or the court clerk to be placed before the judge. By allowing counsel to hand the documents in, he/she will be aware that the document has been lodged and can instantly confirm the same if questioned by the judge.

If the document is not related to the trial you are attending on, the instructing solicitors should tell you where you should hand the documents in. Normally this is either the general office or the listing office.

If unsure take it to the general office and explain that you have been asked to file the document. They will inspect the document and either accept it or point you in the right direction.

When you file a document you do not normally get a receipt. However it is recommended that you obtain a receipt even written on a compliment slip, to confirm that the documents were in fact filed. This should cover you in the event the document should go astray.

Filing/lodging a document therefore simply means that you hand the document in at the court office in order for it to be recorded and placed on the court file.

CHAPTER 22
DISTRICT JUDGE APPLICATION

You may sometimes be called upon to attend before a district judge on a directions appointment hearing. Sometimes the directions hearing is to extend a time limit or to set a time limit for the other party to serve certain documents or perform a certain act. The directions hearing will vary depending on what the particular issue might be.

At such a hearing you will be required to attend and address the district judge without a barrister and make representations with regard to what your instructing solicitors are seeking in their application.

In preparation for the application it is imperative that you are familiar with the case. The district judge may well ask certain questions and if you are familiar with the file you will be able to address that question and present your case with confidence.

If the other side is attending you can seek to try and agree an order before entering the courtroom which the district judge will endorse as a formality if satisfied with its contents.

If your instructing solicitors have made the application you will be the first party to address the district judge. You should address the district judge as Sir or Madam as the case may be.

The district judge may well seek to clarify certain points then give directions making the appropriate order.

These cases are normally listed for about 10 to 15 minutes. You should prepare beforehand what you intend to say to the district judge by way of submissions. Avoid writing everything you wish to say verbatim, but instead make a list of points you wish to address.

If it is your first time and it will make you feel happier you could if time permits write out your submissions in full and then make the list of points from this.

CHAPTER 23
PRISON VISITS

If a client is refused bail and remanded or detained in custody you may be called upon to make a prison visit in order to take instructions. This visit should have been booked well in advance by the instructing solicitors.

Your instructing solicitors should provide you with a letter of introduction addressed to the Governor of the prison, which should contain your name, the name of the client and his prison number and the date and time of the visit. This letter is your authority to attend the prison on behalf of the solicitors. If you do not have the letter with you then you will be refused a visit.

Some prisons are very strict and will only allow you to take the file, writing pad and pens. Everything else should normally be left in a locker. This includes sweets such as mints and in some cases cigarettes. This will however depends on the prison you attend.

If in doubt and to avoid having to leave the prison to return to the locker, you should carry the bare minimum as outlined above or upon arrival at the prison check with the officers what you can or cannot bring. You may find there is a separate entrance for legal visits.

Security

Be prepared to be heavily searched. In some prisons your fingerprints and palm prints will be electronically recorded and you may be recorded on the security camera or your photos taken.

You should also take some means of identification such as a driving licence or passport as you may be asked to prove that you are the person mentioned in the letter of introduction.

If the visit is a conference with counsel you would have been told this before hand and you will meet the barrister at the prison. The barrister will have to go through the same security procedure as you. No one is immune.

Booking-in Procedure

You will be asked to sign in and will then be escorted to the interview area where your client may already be waiting for you. When you leave you will be asked to sign out.

If a client requests that you leave a document from his file this can be done providing the document is in relation to the client's case. Nothing else should be left unless you have been given permission by the prison officers.

If you are asked to attend a prison it is normally either to:

- take a statement
- take instructions on the prosecution statements
- attend a conference with the barrister
- take instruction for bail application
- be present when a statement is taken from client by other officials
- at the client's request

If you have to take a statement then you should follow the procedure outlined. You should bear in mind any particular points, which the instructing solicitors have said need to be clarified.

The statement should contain the following details about the client:

- name and address
- date of birth
- marital status
- client's plea
- client's version of events
- employment details
- family background
- income
- any mitigating circumstances
- medical problems

At the end, the statement should be read back to the client and then he or she should be allowed to sign it.

Always try to build the client's confidence in you by being friendly and relaxed. At the end of the visit summarise what will happen next and ask whether there are any special instructions for the instructing solicitors or whether the client would like messages to be passed to any relatives. Be careful about passing messages. This might involve tipping someone off or assisting someone in a crime. If in doubt do not relay any messages.

CHAPTER 24
LEGAL AID

Legal Aid is public funding granted or loaned to those clients who meet defined eligibility criteria, to assist them in prosecuting or defending a case.

The Legal Aid Board was abolished when the Access to Justice Act came into force in 1999.

This Act brought about major changes to the delivery of legal services throughout England and Wales in both civil and criminal matters.

The main changes are as follows:

- the Legal Services Commission was created

- the Community Legal Service Fund was created

- the legal aid schemes created under the Legal Aid Act 1988 were abolished and replaced with the following two new schemes administered by the Legal Services Commission:

  (i) The Community Legal Service (CLS)
  (ii) The Criminal Defence Service (CDS)

The Act brought to an end the notion that solicitors' practices received remuneration for publicly-funded work as of right. Firms that wish to provide publicly-funded work now have to apply to the Legal Services Commission for approval. This is given in the form of a contract.

By granting this contract, the Legal Services Commission requires firms to work to a certain minimum standard. The standard involves putting in place certain procedures, for example an Office Manual containing the procedures that are followed by the firm to ensure that the client receives a minimum standard of quality service. Firms who satisfy these criteria are allowed to display a Quality Mark and are given preferential treatment. In order to ensure that firms maintain the standard, regular audits are carried out. Firms that fail to keep to the minimum standard risk losing their contract. A firm that does not meet the standard will not be granted a contract.

What is the Legal Services Commission?

The Legal Services Commission (LSC) replaced the Legal Aid Board from 1st April 2000. It is responsible for the administration of a controlled budget known as the Community Legal Service Fund.

The 1999 Act empowers the LSC to identify the need in England and Wales for legal services generally and to plan or provide a solution towards satisfying that need. The aim is that this role should be undertaken in partnership with others, funders and suppliers alike.

The Quality Mark

The Quality Mark is described as the quality standard for legal information, advice and specialist legal services. It comprises a set of standards designed to denote that the service is well run and has its own quality control mechanisms relating to the quality of the information, advice or service a firm provides. Firms who qualify are allowed to display a special symbol which indicates to the public that they have been assessed as reaching the standard necessary to provide quality services, paid for from public funds.

Civil Funding

The Legal Services Commission funds a range of legal services. In civil matters these services are:

Legal Help (LH)

Legal Help replaces the former Green Form scheme sometimes referred to as the Advice and Assistance scheme. Legal Help is administered by the Legal Services Commission.

This scheme allows solicitors to give up to two hours advice and assistance to a client who qualifies under the scheme. Clients who are likely to qualify will have a low income or be in receipt of state benefits. This scheme will cover the solicitor's cost at the first interview of completing the legal aid application for representation at court. As a clerk you may be asked by your instructing solicitors to arrange for a client to sign the LH form on their file. You should double check with the client that the details in the form are correct.

This scheme will not cover representation by a solicitor in court.

Help at Court

Help at Court is the scheme which allows a solicitor or advisor to represent the client at certain court hearings, despite not formerly acting for them in connection with the whole proceedings. This scheme can be used where a matter can be resolved at court that same day.

Approved Family Help

This scheme provides help in relation to a family dispute, including the provision of assistance in resolving that dispute through negotiation or otherwise. This scheme encompasses the services covered by Legal Help, but also includes issuing proceedings, representation where necessary to obtain disclosure of information from another party, or the obtaining of a consent order following agreement of a matter in dispute. It is available in two forms:

(i) Help with Mediation: This includes the provision of legal advice and assistance if the client is attending family mediation.

(ii) General Family Help: The provision of legal advice and assistance on family matters where the client is not attending family mediation.

Family Mediation

The type of service covered by the scheme relates to mediation for a family dispute. This will include the process involved in finding out whether mediation appears to be suitable for the client or not.

Legal Representation

This scheme involves the provision of legal representation in court in the event that the client is taking or defending court proceedings. This was previously called civil legal aid and is available in two forms:

(i) Investigative Help: Funding is limited to the investigation of the strength of a claim.

(ii) Full Representation: Funding is provided to enable representation of the client in legal proceedings.

It is possible for both Investigative Help and Full Representation to be granted on an emergency basis where the matter is urgent and meets the defined criteria.

Conditional Fees Agreement

This is a private arrangement between the client and the solicitor. Usually the parties agree that the client will not pay the solicitor's costs if the client loses the case but this will depend on the nature of the agreement drawn up between the client and the solicitor.

These types of cases were previously paid for by legal aid under the Legal Aid Act 1988.

The Granting of Legal Aid

In civil matters, the document which states that legal aid has been granted is normally referred to as the funding certificate (although many practitioners still refer to it as the legal aid certificate). The funding certificate may be granted on condition that the client pays a contribution. You should check that the contribution has been paid because counsel may well want to know for the purpose of recovering the client's costs, in the event that judgment is made in the client's favour.

Civil legal aid is normally granted subject to limitations. These can only be removed by applying to the Legal Services Commission to amend the certificate.

If the matter has gone to trial the certificate should have been amended to allow the matter to proceed to trial. If the restrictions on the certificate have not been removed it might mean the solicitor would not be paid for any work carried out beyond that specified in the certificate.

In civil matters it should be borne in mind that the legal aid is granted in the form of a loan. Any money or property recovered or preserved can then be used to repay that loan. This is known as the statutory charge. The solicitor should have informed the client about the statutory charge. This simply means that if a client recovers money over a specified sum from the action, some of it will have to be used to repay the legal aid loan. Solicitors or barristers negotiating in respect of ancilliary relief, debt or personal injury matters will need to bear the statutory charge in mind. It is in your client's interest that any negotiations for settlement of a matter take the statutory charge into consideration. You should therefore ask the barrister whether the proposal for settlement has taken the statutory charge into account.

Criminal Legal Funding

Background

The Criminal Defence Service (CDS) replaced the old system of criminal legal aid in April 2001. The purpose of the Criminal Defence Service is to ensure that people suspected or accused of a crime have access to advice, assistance and representation, in the interests of justice.

History

In December 1998 the Government published its plan for reforming legal services and the courts. These plans included the establishment of the Criminal Defence Service to replace the various criminal legal aid schemes in operation at the time.

In July 1999 the Access to Justice Act 1999 received the Royal Assent. This Act created the framework within which the Criminal Defence Service operates, under the management of the Legal Services Commission.

The objectives of the CDS

The CDS aims to:

- ensure that the Government meets its statutory and international obligations to provide that:

    (i) people arrested and held in custody have the right to consult a solicitor in private at any time.

    (ii) defendants have a right to defend themselves in person, or by means of legal assistance of their own choice, or if they have insufficient funds or means to pay for legal assistance, to be given free legal funding if the interests of justice so require.

- help to ensure that suspects and defendants receive a fair hearing at each stage in the criminal justice process and that they can state their case on an equal footing with the prosecution.

- protect the interests of the suspect or the defendant by requiring that the prosecution prove its case or advising the defendant to enter an early guilty plea, if appropriate.

- maintain the defendant or suspect's confidence in the criminal justice system, and to facilitate his or her effective participation in the process.

The Criminal Defence Service (CDS) has a separate budget from the Community Legal Service (CLS) and is a separate scheme. The separation reflects the fact that the two schemes are responsible for providing different types of services in different types of cases and that each scheme has its own objectives and priorities.

The Contribution

If you are attending on a criminal trial there should be on file a Representation Order (legal aid order) granted from the Magistrates' Court to the Crown Court. This will have been extended when the case was committed or transferred to the Crown Court. If a client is acquitted (that is, found not guilty) and has to pay a contribution he may request that the contribution be refunded. You should be familiar with what the Representation Order looks like in the event that Counsel asks you whether the client has to pay a contribution.

In criminal cases the costs of the case should not be an issue. Public funding is available through the Legal Services Commission to ensure that everyone has a fair trial and that justice "is seen to be done".

The Standard Form

Legal aid is applied for by completing a standard form. A statement of means is no longer required in criminal matters. The form will contain the client's name, address, date of birth, the details of the offence, the date he or she has to appear in court and the name of the Magistrates' Court.

If you have to visit the client in prison or to meet him or her at court for the first time, this form can be quite useful in providing a general picture of the client. The other document, which will give you a description of the client, is the custody record.

If for any reason legal aid was not extended from the Magistrates' Court to the Crown Court the barrister can ask the judge to grant legal aid there and then. It will be up to you as the solicitors' representative to complete the legal aid form ensure it is signed by the client and hand it in to the court.

CHAPTER 25
COMPLETIONS

You may be asked to attend on a completion.

The conventional method of completion is for the buyer's solicitors to attend the seller's solicitors' office.

It should be noted however that completions today are normally carried out over the telephone with each solicitor undertaking to forward the documents/payment to each other. Therefore the act of physically attending each other's offices is quite rare.

Completion can be described as the final part of the process in the sale and purchase transaction of a property. It is where the buyer hands over the cheque or banker's draft and the seller hands over the deeds and documents in exchange, together with the keys to the property.

If you are acting for the buyer and are asked to attend on a completion your instructing solicitors should give you full details of the seller's solicitors. This will include their name, address and telephone number including any reference and the name of the other solicitor or representative that you are going to meet. You should check that you have these details.

You will be given a banker's draft which is made out to the seller's solicitors although this will depend on whether there is a mortgage on the property.

You should as a matter of routine, check that the figures on the banker's draft are correct and that it is dated and made out to the correct person.

Your instructing solicitors will give you a list of documents which you should collect.

If they have not done so you should clarify this before leaving the office and make a list of the required documents.

If during the completion you come across any difficulties do not be afraid to contact your instructing solicitors and seek their instructions before proceeding.

If you are acting for the seller after handing over the various documents and keys you will receive the cheque or banker's draft. You should be told by your instructing solicitors what documents should be handed over and if they have not done so you should seek instructions.

Once you have received the banker's draft you should take it to the instructing solicitors as quickly as possible in order for it to be paid into the bank.

The Documents Involved

Some of the documents you may be asked to collect are as follows:

- Conveyance
- Lease
- Assignment
- Transfer
- Land Certificate
- Insurance receipt
- Charge Certificate
- Form 53
- Receipts for ground rent or confirmation of payment
- Guarantee Certificate from the National House Building Association

This is not an exhaustive list and the documents required will depend on whether the transaction concerns a leasehold or freehold property and whether you are acting for the seller or the buyer.

Stamping

You may be called upon by a firm of solicitors to stamp some conveyancing documents. This entails paying a duty (called a stamp duty) on the documents passing title to the purchaser. These could include a transfer, conveyance or lease or other documents such as a stock transfer form.

After the completion of the conveyancing transaction the document passing title to the property should be stamped within 4 weeks with the stamp duty. The documents should also be given an additional stamp called "Particulars Delivered" otherwise known as the PD stamp.

A document does not require stamp duty if it is under a particular threshold (currently £30.000) otherwise stamp duty is payable. Even if there is no stamp duty to be paid however a document may still require a PD stamp.

In London stamping is carried out at Bush House in the Strand London WC2 (opposite Somerset House). At the counter the documents should be presented together with the cheque for the stamp duty.

If there is a problem which you cannot resolve, you will have to report back to your instructing solicitors. If the documents are approved the staff will put the appropriate stamp duty on the document in the form of a seal and you should return the document to your instructing solicitors. If a document is not stamped within the 4 week period then a penalty will become payable.

CHAPTER 26
THE DOCUMENT EXCHANGE SYSTEM (DX)

The document exchange system could be described as an independent postal system where documents posted are guaranteed to reach their destination the next day.

You will find that most solicitors in the London area are members of the document exchange system and their DX number is normally on their letterhead.

It is important to be familiar with the workings of the document exchange system in the event that it is mentioned that documents have been sent via the system.

Firms that are members of the DX system have a box in which letters to them are posted. A member of staff will be responsible for attending daily to collect the letters or documents with a key for their box.

The firms DX box is normally based at a particular exchange point which may be another solicitors' firm.

At the exchange point there is also an outgoing box which is similar to the post box. This is where your letters to other members of the DX will be posted.

CHAPTER 27
DEALING WITH PROBLEMS AT COURT

In the event that problems arise during a hearing you will normally be attending with counsel and counsel should be the one to resolve the problem with your assistance. You should therefore try to be as helpful as possible and be prepared to follow counsel's requests and instructions.

This might mean telephoning the instructing solicitors office, a particular body or other persons. If you are on your own and you believe it is a problem that the office can resolve by a simple telephone call then you should call the office. If you have the file you may be able to obtain the answer from looking through it and therefore phoning the office might be a complete waste of time.

If you are carrying out a task for the first time and you are not sure what to do, the court staff are normally quite helpful. They will also be able to tell you, for example how many copies are required and whether there a fee is payable etc. If a fee is required and no cheque is attached to the file, you will have to contact your instructing solicitors. Upon telephoning the instructing solicitors if you have funds or a cheque book, you could agree to pay the fee on condition that you are reimbursed straight away when you return the file to the office. You should make a note of this for the file and if you are not reimbursed straight away then this should be claimed back when you are submitting your invoice for your services as out of pocket expenses.

Although not an exhaustive list, the problems you may be called upon to deal with at court are as follows:

- the client not attending
- the witness not attending
- confusion over which date a particular witness should attend
- client's surety not in attendance at court
- client changing his instructions at the last minute

- instructing solicitors omitting to file or serve documents
- instructing solicitors' failure to comply with directions
- client unhappy or wishing to dismiss his barrister
- the difficult client who interrupts court proceedings
- client's relatives/friends interrupting proceedings
- threats or intimidation of the client or witnesses
- counsel not in attendance

In resolving most of these problems be prepared to follow counsel's instructions and requests. If you are on your own you will have to use your own initiative and common sense and at the same time be as professional as possible. You must in any event keep your instructing solicitors informed especially if you are on your own and cannot resolve the matter at court. Don't forget to keep an accurate record.

In the event that the barrister does not turn up or is late, you should keep the court informed of the progress you have made in locating counsel. You should have telephoned the instructing solicitors or the barrister's chambers to get an idea of what is holding counsel up.

If you are faced with other problems then as one of the wise clerks who have purchased this book you should be reassured, as it may contain the solution you are looking for!

CHAPTER 28
GENERAL HINTS AND REMINDERS

1. As a general rule you should always arrive at court early. It is recommended that you aim to arrive at least 30 minutes beforehand. However it is appreciated that you may be called upon at short notice in which case not only will you arrive late but you will also not have been able to familiarise yourself with the case. Counsel should already be aware of this, but if he or she is not then you should inform counsel of your position. In order to save time it is recommended that you ask counsel whether he or she wishes to browse through the file to see whether there are anything that he or she would find of assistance which is not already included in the brief.

2. Always prepare pieces of paper to use to write notes to counsel.

3. Always dress smartly. This will give the client confidence in you. Wear dark clothing and if you are a male clerk wear a suit and tie.

4. In matrimonial cases where the husband and wife are estranged or if you are attending an injunction application never let your client sit behind counsel first. You should enter the row of seats behind counsel followed by your client who will be sitting at the end. The reason for this is that in matrimonial cases there might be an element of intimidation and violence from one party to the other. It might be human nature to allow your client to sit down first but if the other legal representative allows their client to do the same this would mean both clients sitting next to each other. This would give one the opportunity to stare and intimidate the other.

    By your entering the row and sitting down first you will act as a barrier between the two thereby preventing any staring or intimidation.

5. Unless you are asked to attend when counsel is discussing the case with the other side's barrister you should always stay with the client. Whatever counsel has discussed will have to be explained to the client in order to take the client's instructions. At this point you will be able to make a note of what was discussed and what was put to the client.

6. Avoid interrupting counsel during a conference unless you can contribute something important or are able to explain counsel's instructions to the client if the client is having difficulty understanding him or her. Be prepared to be rebuffed by counsel if you interrupt without contributing anything of substance.

7. In the event that you arrive early at court always seek to secure a conference room if possible. In a small court these rooms are like gold dust. This will enable counsel and the client to talk in complete privacy without interruption and without people walking past and eavesdropping.

8. Always have change for the phone.

9. Always reassure client where necessary that you and counsel are on his or her side even though the advice may seem to the contrary.

10. If in doubt where to sit when inside the courtroom simply follow counsel. If you are attending a criminal trial the defence normally sit closest to the jury.

11. Under no circumstance should you advise the client. That is counsel's job. You should resist any temptation to do so and if in doubt explain to the client that your job is to assist counsel whose job is to provide the advice.

12. At the end of a criminal case where the client is sentenced to a term of imprisonment, never sign for the client's property which is being held by the police. Arrange for a relative or friend to collect it. Don't forget to ask the client to sign a form of authority for the property to be released to the friend or relative.

13. Always return the file to the instructing solicitors the same day and if not, the next day unless you are instructed otherwise. This will help to keep good relations. If the attendance note is not yet

complete, then you should complete a case summary outlining the order, judgment or decision made at court.

14. In a criminal case under no circumstances should you pass any suspicious messages to the client's friends or relatives whether by phone or in person. You may be assisting in committing a crime.

15. Always bow whenever you enter or leave the courtroom and the judge is sitting. The whole courtroom will be asked to stand whenever the judge enters or leave the courtroom.

16. Always remember to switch off mobile phones to avoid a public rebuke by the judge.

17. At the end of every hearing and in the case of a continuous trial unless you are told otherwise, you should always report back to the instructing solicitors every day to keep them updated on how the hearing is progressing.

CHAPTER 29
THINGS A CLERK MAY BE CALLED UPON TO DO

A clerk may be called upon to do any of the following work:

- Attend the Action Department of the RCJ to issue/file documents
- Attend the Probate Registry to issue, file or attend on queries
- Obtain death/birth/marriage certificates
- Attend before a Practice Master in the High Court
- Obtain Acts of Parliament from HMSO
- Attend a trial/hearing
- Deliver a brief to counsel
- Attend a conference at counsel's chambers
- Arrange for the stamping of conveyancing documents
- Purchase forms from the stationer's
- Collect and deliver post to the DX
- Attend on a prison visit
- Take a statement from a witness
- Carry out research
- Attend and assist in-house
- Attend an immigration interview

CHAPTER 30
CLERKS TOOLS OF TRADE

In order to be fully prepared for clerking, your tools of trade will be the following:

- Briefcase or shoulder bag
- Writing pad, with pens of various colours
- Highlighter
- Pencil and rubber
- Watch
- Coins for the phone
- Mobile phone or pager (if possible)
- Diary (preferably with a calendar)
- This book
- Small A to Z

CHAPTER 31
HOW TO FIND WORK AS A FREELANCE PARALEGAL

Freelance work can be obtained by:

1. Always having business cards printed and ready to hand to solicitors.

2. Writing to local firms in your area to inform them that you are available for work and to ask them to put your name on the list of paralegal clerks they use from time to time. Once you have written the letter you should telephone after about a week to find out whether they have received your letter. (See specimen letter in document section)

3. Telephoning firms to find out whether they use freelance outdoor paralegal clerks. You should concentrate at first on firms that specialise in criminal work because they normally have cases listed at short notice due to the warned list system. Once established in criminal work you can then approach firms that specialise in other areas.

4. Applying to do unpaid work to gain the practical court experience and get your foot in the door of the firm.

5. Registering with Paralegal and Legal Recruitment Agencies once you have some practical experience.

6. Use your knowledge of another language to your advantage by pointing out that you can interpret for a client in that language.

7. Placing an advert in the Law Society's Gazette to advertise your services.

8. Directly approaching local firms to sell yourself to the criminal, family or civil litigation solicitor.

APPENDICES

APPENDIX 1
SPECIMEN FILES

Case Study A – Criminal

IN THE STREATHAM CROWN COURT	No: T 951234

LEGAL AID

BETWEEN:

REGINA

– AND –

ROMEO JONES

BRIEF TO COUNSEL

Counsel has herewith copies of the following:

1. **Draft indictment**
2. **Proof of Evidence**
3. **Bundle of Committal Statements**
4. **Custody Record***
5. **Previous Convictions***
6. **Tape X3***
7. **Comments on Prosecution Statements**
8. **Witness Statements**

---

*   not included

1. Counsel is instructed on behalf of the Defendant Romeo Jones, born the 23rd April 1940 and resides at 25 Mitcham Road, London SW12.

Charge

2. Counsel is referred to the draft indictment and will note that the Defendant is charged with:

    (1) ABH contrary to Section 47 of the Offences Against the Persons Act 1961; and

    (2) intimidation contrary to Section 5(1) of the Criminal Justice and Public Order Act 1994.

Proceedings to Date

3. The Defendant last appeared at the Walworth Green Magistrates' Court on the 13th January 2000 when he was committed for trial to Streatham Crown Court under Section 6(2) of the Magistrates' Court Act 1980. The Plea and Directions hearing was fixed for 20th February 2000.

Plea

4. The Defendant intends to plead Not Guilty to these charges.

Bail

5. The Defendant is on Conditional Bail not to contact the Prosecution Witnesses directly or indirectly.

Details of Offence

6. The Prosecution case is that on the 24th of April 1999 the alleged victim who is the Defendant's wife, was at home with the Defendant.

7. It was the Defendant's birthday and his wife had prepared a meal which she took into the sitting-room where the Defendant was watching TV. The Defendant's feet were on the table and his wife asked him to move his feet but he ignored her. After asking the Defendant two or three times to move his feet his wife placed the food next to his feet at which point the Defendant became furious and stood up and shouted to his wife "Don't you respect me?".

8. The Defendant is alleged to have then grabbed the victim by her neck with both hands and tried to strangle her. In the struggle she fell on the tray of food and then onto the settee.

9. She was then hit in the right eye and started to scream and their two sons came into the room and tried to calm the Defendant down.

10. His wife, the victim, noticed she was bleeding from her neck. She was feeling dizzy and her son helped her to sit down and then called the emergency doctor at around 2am.

11. She did not call the police straightaway as she was too ill and when she went to her doctor she was told to report the matter to the police. Her GP also gave her a letter to attend Prince Albert Hospital which she did and then reported the matter to the police.

12. In April 1999 the victim obtained new safe accommodation in order to get away from the Defendant.

13. As regards the alleged intimidation, on the 15th October the victim attended Walworth Green Magistrates' Court to give evidence in relation to the death of her daughter in a Road Traffic Accident.

14. The Defendant and his brother were present at Court and after the hearing the Defendant is alleged to have told the victim "that she should reconcile and then they can make a case against the woman who caused their daughter's death".

15. The Defendant is alleged to have said "if you don't withdraw the criminal case then I can't help you to bring a proper legal case against the lady who killed our daughter. If you don't withdraw the case and I go to prison then when I come back I will do you".

16. The defendant's brother then went over to the Defendant and took an envelope from him and gave it to the victim. His brother said "here is £100 for you and the children". The victim then said "No, Romeo is a cheat, I will not accept any money from him".

17. The victim then complained that she had not received any money since February 2000 regarding Child Benefit and when she tried to tell his brother the Defendant became angry and was told by his brother to leave the room.

18. For further details Counsel is referred to the victim's statement.

19. For details of the Defendant's version of events Counsel is referred to his proof of evidence.

Points to Note

20. Counsel should note that the Defendant was originally charged with two counts of ABH.

21. Counsel will also note from the Defendant's proof of evidence that he claims his wife suffers from depression as a result of her diabetes and needs counselling. He also states that his wife was admitted to the Prince Albert Hospital Psychiatric Ward, due to her tendency to harm herself. Counsel is referred to the letter from their Doctor dated 9th November which confirms that she suffers from diabetes but has never received psychiatric treatment as a result.

22. With regards to the intimidation of the witness, the Defendant completely denies this and states in the interview that he was merely giving her money for maintenance since his wife was complaining that he had not given her any money. At the time of dictating these instructions the Instructing

Solicitors will be seeking to obtain a statement from the Defendant's brother who was present.

23. This matter has been listed for Pleas and Directions on the 20th February 2000 at 10am and should Counsel feel that a conference is required prior to that hearing please do not hesitate to contact Victor Good of the Instructing Solicitors in order to arrange a suitable time.

24. Counsel is instructed accordingly.

V. Good & Co. Solicitors
06/01/00

Proof of Evidence

[_____]

NAME: ROMEO JONES

ADDRESS: 25 MITCHAM ROAD, LONDON SW12

DATE OF BIRTH: 23/04/40

OCCUPATION: NURSING ASSISTANT

Romeo Jones will say:

I have been charged with ABH on my wife to which I intend to plead not guilty. The circumstances leading to this alleged assault are as follows:

On the 23rd April 1999 in the morning, at about 9.30am, I reminded my wife that it was my birthday that day and that it was St George's day. We are a Christian family and must therefore pray. I also said that we should remember the soul of our departed daughter who died in a road traffic accident and whom we had recently buried.

My wife replied by saying "Your birthday, so what?". I immediately realised that she was not in a good mood. I told her that I would be going window-shopping in Balham. I then left the house about 10.30am and went to Balham until about 4pm.

From there I went to visit a family friend in Croydon. I left there about 7pm and arrived home about 9pm.

On arrival I went straight into the living room and sat down after saying hello to my wife and my two sons who were there. I then told my wife that our family friends sent their love. She immediately "flared up" and said angrily, in a loud voice "Yes you went to celebrate your birthday with your friends". I told her that this was not the case. I explained that after window-shopping I decided to go and say hello to them and did not even mention my birthday until I was saying goodbye because I was not celebrating it anyway.

I then asked the children whether they had eaten already and they said they had. I then asked my wife whether she had prepared any meal for me. She did not answer me. I waited for about an hour and then I asked my second son to buy me cod and chips from the chip shop.

On his return I ate the fish and chips and I listened to the news. By this time both my sons and my wife had left the living-room. I sat on the settee with my feet on the table when suddenly I felt my feet being pushed off the table. I regained my balance and turned to see it was my wife holding a plate of food on a tray in one hand and using the other hand to push my feet away. I should add that I did not see her coming into the room as my back was to the door.

Whilst still sitting I asked her why she couldn't say excuse me or show a little respect to me. She then shoved the plate in my face and said "where else do you think I should put this food?".

In order to prevent the tray with a plate from hitting my face I pushed her onto the three-seater settee behind her and stood up at the same time.

She then started shouting calling the boys and I started to walk towards the bedroom. As the boys entered the room she removed her shoe and threw it at me, at the same time telling the boys she had bought my meal to me and I pushed her away. Whilst telling the boys this she lunged at me when she realised the shoe had missed and my sons had to pull her back.

I then rushed into the bedroom and locked the door to avoid any further contact.

She came to the room and started banging on the door and shouting abuse at me.

I was talking and watching her through the keyhole and told her to calm down as we were in a state of mourning. She became hysterical, pulling her hair and running her fingers through her hair about her neck and stamping. This went on for about two hours before she calmed down.

When she calmed down I came out of the bedroom and she was lying on the sofa crying. I could see her eyes had swollen from the crying and told her she should take her diabetic tablets and eat something. She did not answer. She told me she was not feeling very well. I told her that was even more reason for her to take her medication and eat something.

Before I had come out of the room she had told my sons to call the emergency doctor. The doctor came and I explained that she had upset herself over an argument and had not eaten or taken her medication.

The doctor examined her and gave her a prescription and she gave it to my son to go to the chemist in Streatham. I gave him £5 for his fare.

After the doctor left my wife had calmed down even more and I talked to her explaining that we should not be fighting as we are in a state of mourning for our daughter. After taking her medication she slept.

In the morning she went to the GP instead of the hospital and I stayed with the baby.

Sometime after that she left and went to a new address with the boys.

Between this time and my arrest things had calmed down and I was surprised when on the 21st August 1999 the police came to my house and arrested me.

I was taken to Balham Police Station where I was questioned in a taped interview and charged and bailed to attend Court.

I should add that between the incident and arrest my wife had taken out an injunction against me in respect of which I did not attend Court.

Under no circumstances did I assault my wife or cause those injuries which I believe were self-inflicted when she became hysterical when I was watching her through the keyhole and talking to her.

The injuries could also have been caused by my sons who had to restrain her.

With regard to my background I was born in Birmingham and moved to London in 1986 to study. My wife and two sons moved down the following year.

I have three boys and one girl recently killed in a road traffic accident. The three remaining are aged 20, 17 and two years old. Our daughter who died would have been eight.

I have been married to my wife for 21 years and I am a nursing assistant earning £300 per week of which I pay £85 per week in rent and the rest in bills.

I would describe myself as healthy. I have previous convictions for motoring offences.

I would like to emphasise that my wife needs medical treatment and counselling because of her past and present diabetic complications, joint pains, depression and delusions for which she repeatedly states that people around her want to harm her. She started drinking excessively after the funeral to date and has developed a tendency to talking about the same subject for two to three hours non-stop.

I am particularly concerned for my wife's emotional behaviour as she went as far as to even accuse me of killing our daughter when she knew I was at work before the killer driver struck her with the unforgettable death-blow. This has caused me emotional torment for which I have been receiving counselling from my doctor and the hospital chaplain where I work.

Between 1995 and 1997 she was admitted to Prince Albert Hospital for her diabetic condition and there was a time when she was admitted to the psychiatric ward due to her tendency of trying to harm herself.

In the Streatham Crown Court   No: T 951234

Between:

Regina

– and –

Romeo Jones

Statement **of** **Alan Jones**

I MR ALAN JOHN JONES OF 24 UPPER STREET LONDON N.1. Date of birth 11 March 1938, Mechanic, MAKE THIS STATEMENT KNOWING THAT IT COULD BE USED IN COURT AND THAT I COULD BE PROSECUTED IF I HAVE STATED ANYTHING THAT IS FALSE OR THAT I DO NOT BELIEVE TO BE TRUE.

SIGNED _____ DATED _____

I am the brother of Mr Romeo Jones and a senior member of The Holy Trinity Church. I am sometimes called upon as an intermediary when there is a problem to try to resolve the matter and my word carries a lot of weight and respect. I am sometimes called upon to act as a peacemaker to try and resolve any problem before it gets out of hand and also to try and sort it out privately rather than in the public eye.

I am aware of the full history of the problem between Romeo and his wife Juliet and that Romeo has been charged with ABH and the intimidation of a witness.

In January 1999 I was called upon by Romeo as a result of an argument between him and his wife. Romeo complained that at times his wife became very verbally abusive towards him and his family life was deteriorating in that Juliet was not helping out around the house or supporting him, nor was she encouraging the children in their chores around the house and their school work. I spoke to Juliet several times about this and encouraged her to support her husband a bit more.

With regard to her aggressive behaviour I told her that if she had a problem she could contact me and I would try to resolve it. I gave her my telephone number. She did ring me a few times complaining that Romeo had not been helping her financially. She said that whenever she gets welfare benefits Romeo would make use of them. I called Romeo about this and he said that all the money he gets is spent on the house and buying food for the children. I also understand that Romeo was getting additional help from the DSS as a carer for his wife when she was very ill. She complained that Romeo was not spending money on her and threatened to stop it.

About the 1st June 1999 I was called upon by both Romeo and Juliet to discuss the current problem that they had been having in the family. Juliet accused Romeo of killing their daughter Jeanette who died in a road traffic accident. She also accused Romeo of attempting to strangle her in the car. I asked her in which way he tried to strangle her but she refused to answer. I repeated the question a few times but she did not reply. I also asked her in which way Romeo killed their daughter Jeanette and she said that when the driver ran over Jeanette and killed her, Romeo was not crying and she felt strongly that it was Romeo who killed Jeanette.

There was also an argument about their birthdays. Juliet complained that on Romeo's previous birthday she took him and the children to have a meal and yet when it was her birthday Romeo did nothing. At another meeting Juliet complained that on Romeo's last birthday he did not stay at home but went off to Croydon. She complained that she had made a meal for him and tried to put it on the table. Romeo was resting his feet on the table and Juliet was trying to put the meal on the table next to his feet. She complained that Romeo kicked the food off the table. Romeo explained to me that he did not kick the food deliberately but Juliet insisted that he did.

I explained to them that these were all petty arguments and Juliet kept going on and on about it and would not accept what was being said. Eventually Romeo apologised and explained that it was not done deliberately but Juliet would still not accept that.

I should add that previously I had told Romeo that whenever a dispute or argument was getting out of hand he should leave the room or the house and allow things to cool down. Romeo has told me that he has done that on previous occasions but Juliet simply followed and insulted him.

At no stage in my presence did Juliet complain that Romeo had tried to strangle her regarding the incident of the meal and his feet on the table. The only time she mentioned being strangled was when she was in the car, which she refused to expand on.

With regards to the witness intimidation on the 15th October 2000, on this day I attended Walworth Green Magistrates' Court regarding the hearing involving the motorist who ran over Jeanette. I arrived at Court about 10.45am. I saw Juliet and Romeo in the courtroom together. After 30 minutes the case was adjourned and we came out. Juliet was very distressed and Romeo comforted her. Another solicitor was also comforting her.

Later we went to a shop to purchase some drinks and we went back to the Court and Romeo and Juliet sat next to each other. I was sitting at the back. After the verdict Juliet started to cry because the driver was only fined and her licence endorsed and Romeo and his solicitor comforted her. Juliet went straight to Romeo for comfort and was very distressed and started to pull her hair and scratch her face. The solicitor spoke to her and then we left. Romeo and myself were making our way to the bus stop and Juliet followed without being invited. We took the bus and went to Romeo's house, arriving about 3.30pm. Juliet started to cry again and Romeo comforted her once more.

I knew about the injunction against Romeo that he should not contact her directly or indirectly and I asked Juliet if I could greet her because I did not want to offend the injunction. She agreed to this. I spoke to her and asked about the children. All of a sudden she started talking about all that had happened previously and kept going on and on and accused Romeo of killing Jeanette because he did not cry.

She complained about what had happened in the past and said she had been coming to see Romeo. On one occasion when she came it was to make peace with Romeo. Romeo called the police because she was hostile to him and he was afraid of being accused of doing something to her.

Later Romeo prepared a meal and she complained it was cold. She suggested that Romeo should heat the meal which he did. Romeo bought some beers for us to drink. After we had prayed Juliet and I each had a beer. Romeo told her that she should not drink the beer because of her diabetes and her doctor had told her not to drink alcohol. She took not notice and had the beer anyway. Later I gave Juliet £10 for her fare and when Romeo came in from the kitchen she told him that he should thank me for the £10.

Later she accused Romeo of not sending the children money and Romeo disputed that saying he had sent money on two occasions. I told her that when we went to Court once or twice I saw Romeo with a cheque and £100 and I wanted to know whether Romeo had given it to her. She said no money was given to her. I said that I had seen Romeo showing a cheque and £100 to his solicitors and had shown me shopping purchased for the children. Romeo intervened and said that he had even got the cheque and money with him. I asked Romeo for the money and said to Juliet that she needed the money for food. I reminded her that she had been complaining that she had no money for food, a fridge and a cooker etc. She refused to take the money. I asked her to accept some food but again she refused.

Juliet said that she wanted to go and I offered to accompany her to the bus stop with a bag of shopping and the money, but she would not accept the money. I told her that if she did not want the money she should at least take the shopping but she refused.

At no stage in my presence did Romeo offer his wife any money to stop the criminal case and I am willing to attend Court to say this if necessary.

SIGNED _____ **DATED** _____

Example of an Indictment

IN THE STREATHAM CROWN COURT   No.

INDICTMENT

THE QUEEN v ROMEO JONES

ROMEO JONES is charged as follows:

Count 1

STATEMENT OF OFFENCE

ASSAULT OCCASIONING ACTUAL BODILY HARM, contrary to Section 47 of the Offences Against the Person Act 1961

PARTICULARS OF OFFENCE

ROMEO JONES on a day between 23rd day of April 1999 and the 26th day of April 1999 assaulted Juliet JONES thereby occasioning her actual bodily harm.

Count 2

STATEMENT OF OFFENCE

INTIMIDATION, contrary to Section 5(1) of the Criminal Justice and Public Order Act 1994

PARTICULARS OF OFFENCE

ROMEO JONES on the 15 day of October 2000 at Walworth Green Magistrates' Court did an act which intimidated Juliet JONES knowing that she was a witness in proceedings for a offence and intending thereby to cause the course of justice to be obstructed, perverted or interfered with.

Officer of the Court

Example Only

STREATHAM CROWN COURT   No.

BETWEEN:

REGINA

v

ROMEO JONES

	COMMITTAL STATEMENTS

1	Juliet JONES	7.6.99	1–2
2	Anthony JONES	17.7.99	3–5
3	Mr G.P. WHO	20.8.99	6
4	PC Donald DIXON	28.8.99	7–8
5	PC Donald DIXON	27.9.99	9
6	Juliet JONES	16.10.99	10–11
7	Donald DIXON	1.11.99	12–13
8	Donald DIXON	18.10.99	14
9	Donald DIXON	7.11.99	15

Example

Witness Statement

(CJ Act 1967, s.9 MC Act 1980, s.102 MC Rules 1981 r.70)

Statement of JULIET JONES

Age if under 21   'over 21'   (If over 21 insert 'over 21')
Occupation   Unemployed

This statement (consisting of 2 pages each signed by me) is true to the best of my knowledge and belief and I make it knowing that, if it is tendered in evidence, I shall be liable to prosecution if I have wilfully stated in it anything which I know to be false or do not believe to be true.

Dated   7th June 1999

Signature   J Jones

On the 24th April 1999 I was at my home address in the company of my ex-husband Romeo Jones. Although we are legally separated from each other he was staying with me at my home. At about midnight it was his birthday, we had recently had a tragic death in the family. Our daughter was killed in a road traffic accident. We were in the process of organising funeral arrangements, I had prepared a meal for Romeo's birthday. When the food was ready I went into the sitting-room. He was watching the telly. He had his feet on the table where I was going to present the food. I asked him to move his feet, he ignored me. I then asked him again two or three times. I then put the tray with the food next to his feet. He then became very furious. He stood up and began to shout at me, "Don't you respect me?". He then grabbed me around the neck with both hands, he was trying to strangle me. He had a very tight grip around my neck. I felt I was suffocating. I could not breath. In the struggle he pushed me I landed on the tray and fell onto the settee. I don't know what happened then but I was hit in the right eye which caused me to go dizzy. I was screaming and my boys came into the sitting-room. The boys were asking what was wrong. They tried to calm him down. I then noticed that I was bleeding from my neck. I got a tissue to stop the bleeding. When I was struck in the eye I could not see clearly and it was watering a lot. My eldest son held me and sat me down on the chair in the sitting-room. He saw that I was feeling dizzy and I told him I could not see properly from my eye. My son called the emergency doctor who came at about 2 am. At the time I did not call the police immediately because I was feeling too ill. I then went to my doctor, then he explained I should report this matter to the police. I am currently a diabetic and I was feeling too shocked. My son went to the 24 hours chemist to collect a prescription which was given to me by the emergency doctor that evening. My GP then gave me a letter to attend Prince

Albert Hospital which I did. I then decided to report this matter to the police as I had suffered violent attacks before from my ex-husband, which was the reason for us separating. In April the council gave me new safe accommodation in order to get away from my violent husband. I had the keys in my handbag to this property. I had hidden these from him because I did not want him to know my new address. He must have searched through my handbag which was hidden away. He stole the keys from out of my handbag. He must have looked in my bag for the new address. He then went to my new address let himself inside and was met by my eldest son Anthony. Romeo then told my son to leave. He then slept in my bed and waited for me to return home.

I didn't go home that night I stayed with a friend. He then left the next day and went back to our old address (over). My son Anthony told me that his dad had went around to the new address and stayed in order to wait for me coming home. I then asked him for the keys. He would not give me them he started to become violent and I came into Balham Police Station with my son to report the matter about the keys. I was advised to come and speak to PC Dixon who is dealing with this matter. I did not give my ex-husband permission to take my house keys or enter my new private address. I am willing to go to court and give evidence in this matter if necessary.

Signature: J. JONES   Signature Witnessed by: PC DIXON PC 316 MD

Example

Witness Statement

(CJ Act 1967, s.9 MC Act 1980, s.102 MC Rules 1081, r.70)

Statement of Anthony JONES

Age if under 21   19 years (If over 21 insert 'over 21')
Occupation   unemployed

This statement (consisting of: 3 pages each signed by me) is true to the best of my knowledge and belief and I make it knowing that, if it is tendered in evidence, I shall be liable to prosecution if I have wilfully stated in it anything which I know to be false or do not believe to be true.

Dated: 17th July 1999

Signature: Anthony Jones

I am nineteen years of age and the oldest out of 3 children. I have two brothers, one age 17 and the other age 2 years old. I live with my mum in a flat belonging to a Housing Association (address is known to the police). We used to live at 25 Mitcham Road, SW12 with my father but he assaulted my mother on 24th April 1999 and so we had to leave the home because my mum was so frightened of him. I witnessed my dad doing this and I will tell you what happened. The assault occurred in the early hours of the 24th April 1999 but the evening before my mum and myself and 2 brothers were sitting at home waiting for my dad to come home. It was his birthday and he'd been out celebrating. It had gone 10 pm and my 2 brothers had gone to bed. My mother by now had gone to the kitchen to do some cooking for the family and I was watching "Sky" television in the sitting-room. I heard the front door open and knew that it was my dad coming home. Dad come into the sitting room and sat down. He did not say hello which is normal. I then went into my bedroom because I felt that dad was not in a good mood. I could tell this because he wasn't talking much even though it was his birthday. I listened to my radio in bed and then fell asleep. I was woken by the sounds of my mum screaming. It was coming from next door which is the sitting-room. I don't know what the time was but I guess it was in the early hours of the morning of the 24th. I went into the living-room. The lights were off but the television was still on and I could see my dad pinning my mother down on the long sofa in the sitting-room. He had his hands around her neck and he looked like he was strangling her. My mum was waving her arms around wildly. My dad had his back to me so he didn't see me come in. I rushed over to him and put both of my arms around his chest and dragged him off my mum. As soon as he saw it was me he stopped trying to strangle her. He then said "You should warn your mother she's getting on my nerves". I asked him what happened. He said "I was busy minding my own business watching TV and your mother come in and pulled a table from under my legs". I know that my mother had been cooking my dad's meal in the kitchen earlier and she probably wanted the table to put his food on. I said "So that's your reason for getting angry". My mum was now shouting at my dad saying "There's no reason for you doing anything to me today, so don't take your anger out on me". I noticed that mum had some marks around her neck and there was a little bit of blood on her neck and she was complaining about pains in her neck and other parts of her body. She said she felt sick so we called an emergency doctor this was later on in the day. I didn't call the police when my dad did this, neither did my mum. I don't remember my dad apologising to my mum but when the GP arrived in the evening my dad told him that my mum had an infection and a sore eye.

I could see that her left eye was swollen and red. The doctor gave my mum a prescription and I went to a pharmacy in Streatham which was a late night pharmacy. I have lived in London since the age of 10 and my dad has always beaten my mum. She normally has swellings and aches from his beatings. He's tried to strangle her 3 or 4 times before but the police have never been called to any of her beatings. My mum has not wanted to call the police before because she tried to sort it out with our Uncle. What I mean is someone within the family but this last incident has been too much for her. I would be willing to go to court and give evidence to support my mum. My dad has not been very good to my mother especially when she fell ill due to her gallstones. She was neglected by my father which was really bad because she was sick for 3 years with this and had several operations.

Anthony Jones   PC Dixon

Signature: A Jones   Signature Witnessed by: PC Dixon

Example

Witness Statement

(CJ Act 1967, s.9 MC Act 1980, s.102, MC Rules 1981, r. 70)

Statement of   DR... George P. Who

Age if under 21   'over 21' (if over 21 insert 'over 21').

Occupation   Doctor

This statement (consisting of 1 page each signed by me) is true to the best of my knowledge and belief and I make it knowing that, if it is tendered in evidence, I shall be liable to prosecution if I have wilfully stated in it anything which I know to be false or do not believe to be true.

Dated   the 20th day of AUGUST 1999

Signature   DR   GP Who

I am a medical practitioner currently employed as a Senior Registrar in the Accident and Emergency Department of Prince Albert Hospital. I saw Mrs Juliet Jones of 25 Mitcham Road, SW12 after her presentation to A&E at 15.06. Her presenting complaint was of alleged assault. On examination she was anxious but otherwise neurologically normal. She had two parallel 3 cm x 1 cm abrasions over her mid-sternomastoid on her left side, with a surrounding 5 cm x 8 cm bruise. The patient had reduced range of all movements in her neck, most marked with flexion and rotation to the right. I also noted bilateral conjuctival injection. Facial examination revealed swelling and tenderness over her right cheek. She had a small abrasion on her left thumb. Mrs Juliet Jones was given painkillers and advised to seek further care from her local practitioner.

DR George P. Who

Signature DR George P. Who   Signature witnessed by

Example

Witness Statement

(CJ Act 1967, s.(MC Act 1980, s.102 MC Rules 1981, r.70)

Statement of   PC Donald Dixon

Age if under 21   'over 21' (If over 21 insert 'over 21')

Occupation   Police Officer

This statement (consisting of 2 pages each signed by me) is true to the best of my knowledge and belief and I make it knowing that, if it is tendered in evidence, I shall be liable to prosecution if I have wilfully stated anything in it which I know to be false or do not believe to be true.

Dated   28 day of AUGUST 1999

Signature   Donald Dixon

On Tuesday the 26th June 1999 at about 08.48am I was on duty in plain clothes attached to the Community Support Group Unit at Balham Police Station. I was investigating an allegation made of an Actual Bodily Harm to a Mrs Juliet Jones by her ex-husband Mr Romeo Jones of 25 Mitcham Road SW12. This alleged assault occurred on the 24th April 1999 at the above address. Mr Jones tried to strangle his ex-wife and punched her in the eye causing injuries amounting to Actual Bodily Harm. I attended this address in possession of her statement made on the 7th June 1999. I was in company with PC 121 and PC 212 who drove in a marked police van. We all attended the address which was on the ground floor. A man answered the door and confirmed his identity as Mr Romeo Jones having the date of birth 23/04/40. We all went into the living-room and I put the allegation to Mr Jones. He said "I didn't assault anyone". I then cautioned him at 8.05am and arrested him for Actual Bodily Harm. He replied "It was a Birthday, she said it was a Birthday". He then dressed and was placed in a marked police van together with myself and conveyed to Balham Police Station. I made the record of the earlier conversation whilst en route. There were no incidents in the van. At Balham Police Station the facts were relayed to PS 22 Bob the Custody Sergeant. Mr Jones was then booked in and offered refreshments and searched. Mr Jones was then interviewed on tape between 09.38 and 10.00am and denied assaulting his wife but admitted pushing her though. He stated that the marks to her neck were superficial and caused by herself. He was then bailed to return to Balham Police Station for 30/07/99 at 11.00am. On Wednesday 21st August 1999 at about 11am Mr Jones returned on bail after being re-bailed. He was further interviewed on tape re: a further allegation of assault on his wife. Between the times of 12.40 and 12.55 Mr Jones denied assaulting his wife on that occasion. He stated that it was an accident. He was then charged with two cases of assault at 12pm. His reply to the caution was

"I didn't assault Juliet, she's my wife, she's a good wife". His fingerprints, photographs and DNA mouth swabs were taken. He was then bailed to attend Walworth Green Magistrates' Court on 27th September 1999 at 09.45am.

Signature PC Donald Dixon   Signature witnessed by

Example

Witness statement

(CJ Act 1967, s.9 MC Act 1980, s.102 MC Rules 1981, r.70)

Statement of   D. Dixon

Age if under 21   'Over 21' (If over 21 insert 'over 21')

Occupation   Police Constable

This statement (consisting of 1 page each signed by me) is true to the best of my knowledge and belief and I make it knowing that, if it is tendered in evidence, I shall be liable for prosecution if I have wilfully stated in it anything which I know to be false or do not believe to be true.

Dated: 27th September 1999

Signature   PC D Dixon

On the 26th June 1999 between 9.38am and 10.00am I interviewed Romeo Jones on tape. Later a transcript was made of this interview which I identify with the mark DD/1A. Then on the 21st August 1999 between the times of 12.40pm and 12.55pm I further interviewed Mr Jones on tape and I identify the transcript as identify mark DD/2A. I exhibit the interview tape made on 26th June 1999 as DD/1 and exhibit the tape of the second interview made on 21st August 1999 as DD/2.

Donald Dixon

Signature PC Donald Dixon   Signature witnessed by

Example

Witness Statement

CJ Act 1967, s.9 MC Act 1980, s.102 MC Rules 1981, r.70)

Statement of   Mrs Juliet Jones

Age if under 21   'Over 21' (If over 21 insert 'over 21')

Occupation   Housewife

This statement (consisting of: 1 pages each signed by me) is true to the best of my knowledge and belief and I make it knowing that, if it is tendered in evidence, I shall be liable to prosecution if I have wilfully stated anything which I know to be false or do not believe to be true.

Dated   16th October 1999

Signature   J Jones

Further to my statement already made to the police. I would like to add that since the death of my daughter Jeanette I have been involved with the case and I had to attend Walworth Green Magistrates' Court yesterday the 15th October 1999 to give evidence in my belated daughter's case. My husband Romeo Jones was also there with his brother. After the court case yesterday my husband Romeo said to me "I should reconcile with him and then we can make a case against the woman who killed our daughter." Romeo then said "if you don't withdraw the criminal case then I can't help you to make a legal case against the lady who killed Jeanette. If you don't withdraw the case and I go to prison then when I come back I will do you". Romeo said this to try to scare me. Then his brother went over to Romeo and took an envelope from him and tried to give me the envelope. His brother said "Here's £100 for you and the children". I said "No Romeo is a cheat I will not accept any money from him". I know that Romeo is working as a nurse in hospital. Since February 2000 I have not received any money from him for the children. When I tried to tell the brother what had been going on with me and Romeo, Romeo become angry and I thought he was going to hit me so his brother told him to leave the room. This brother knows that he was a violent man from before but he still said to me to withdraw the case against Romeo. I will not because he should not get away with it. Romeo has already told my sons not give evidence against him. He is very clever with words and has brainwashed the children.

Signature: Juliet Jones   Signature witnessed by

Example

Witness Statement

(CJ Act 1967, s.9 MC Act 1980, s.102 MC Rules 1981, r.70)

Statement by Donald Dixon

Age if under 21 'Over 21' (If over 21 insert 'over 21')

Occupation   Police Officer

This statement (consisting of 1 pages each signed by me) is true to the best of my knowledge and belief and I make it knowing that, if it is tendered in evidence, I shall be liable for prosecution if I have wilfully stated anything which I know to be false or do not believe to be true.

Dated: 1st November 1999

Signature: Donald Dixon

On the 18th October 1999 at about 16.05pm I was on duty in plain clothes attached to the Community Support Unit at Balham Police Station. I was in possession of a statement made by a Mrs Juliet Jones alleging her husband Romeo Jones had tried to bribe her at Walworth Green Magistrates' Court to drop the criminal proceedings against her husband for which I am the original officer in the case. Whilst at court for criminal proceedings regarding the death of her daughter, her husband Romeo Jones had given an envelope to his brother to give Juliet Jones. The envelope contained £100. He told her to drop the case otherwise they would not get compensation for the death of her daughter. He also threatened to assault her if he went to prison. I attended Mr Jones address of 25 Mitcham Road SW12 with a uniformed officer driving a marked police vehicle. At the address Mr Jones, who I recognised from previous dealings with him, asked us to come into his flat. I then explained to him why I was there and repeated the allegation to him and cautioned him. He made no reply. I therefore arrested him at 17.00 for witness intimidation and trying to pervert the course of justice. He made no reply to the caution. He went over to the table and picked up a cheque (DD/10) serial no:– 01011959 made payable to Juliet Jones for the amount of £100 dated 26/9/99. He also had an envelope which later was found to contain £100 in £20 notes. On the inside of the envelope it read "Juliet for you, take care of the baby, God bless", signed Romeo dated 26/9/99 (DD/11). These items were later kept by police. Mr Jones was then conveyed to Balham Police Station, where the facts were relayed to the custody sergeant.

Signature: Donald Dixon   Signature witnessed by:

Example

Witness Statement

(CJ Act 1967, s.9 MC Act 1980, s.102 Rules 1981, r.70)

Statement of   PC Donald Dixon

Age if under 21   'Over 21' (If over 21 insert 'over 21')

Occupation   Police Officer

This statement (consisting of 1 page each signed by me) is true to the best of my knowledge and belief and I make it knowing that, if it is tendered in evidence, I shall be liable to prosecution if I have wilfully stated in it anything which I know to be false or do not believe to be true.

Dated: 18 of October 1999

Signature: PC Donald Dixon

On the 18th October 1999 between the times of 18.04pm and 18.55pm I interviewed the defendant on tape and the tape of this interview I identify with the mark DD/1 and the transcript of this tape will be identified with the mark DD/2.

Signature: P C Donald Dixon   Signature witnessed by

Example

Witness Statement

(CJ Act 1967, s.9 MC Act 1980, s.102 Rules 1981, r.70)

Statement of   Donald Dixon

Age if under 21   'Over 21' (If over 21 insert 'over 21')

Occupation   Police Officer

This statement (consisting of 1 page each signed by me) is true to the best of my knowledge and belief and I make it knowing that, if it is tendered in evidence, I shall be liable to prosecution if I have wilfully stated in it anything which I know to be false or do not believe to be true.

Dated: 7 November 1999

Signature: Donald Dixon

On the 18th of October 1999 I was on duty in plain clothes attached to the Community Support Unit at Balham Police Station. I was in the Custody Suite and at 19.26 I was present whilst Mr Romeo Jones was charged with witness intimidation and trying to pervert the course of justice. He made no reply to the caution.

Donald Dixon

Signature: Donald Dixon   Signature witnessed by

R v Romeo Jones

Defendant's Comments on Prosecution Statements

1st Witness of Juliet Jones

Dated 7th June 1999

Line 1–10

I am not her ex-husband as we are still married nor are we legally separated. In any event the 23rd April was my birthday and not the 24th.

Although I accept that later food was brought in, on arrival home I asked her whether there was any food and she did not answer me. As a result I sent my son to buy fish and chips.

It was after this that she came in and pushed me feet off the table without saying a word.

I was not furious and nor did I say "Don't you respect me?". I said "Can't you say excuse me or show some respect for your husband?".

I dispute that I had my hands around her neck and was trying to strangle her.

Line 11–13

There was no struggle whatsoever. What she did was to push the tray and plate of food into my face and at the same time saying "where else do you think I should put this food?".

As a reflex action, to avoid the food being pushed into my face, I pushed her and she fell on the settee behind her. She did not land on the tray as she claimed. It is a complete and utter lie that I hit her in the eye.

Line 14–16

She was not screaming but she was calling the boys who were next door. They did not try and calm me down, they tried to calm her down. At that point she took off her shoe and threw it at me. I ducked and ran and locked myself in the bedroom.

As far as I am aware there was no bleeding before I locked myself in the bedroom. If that was the case the boys would have seen the bleeding when they tried to calm her down and if so they would have been very angry with me.

Any bruises would have been caused by her when she became hysterical when I locked myself in the room.

Line 17–20

I cannot comment as I was locked in the bedroom. Before the doctor came she had calmed down and I came out of the bedroom. I apologised and told her she had upset herself for nothing because with my back turned to the door I could not see her holding anything or I would have moved my feet from the table.

She then replied that she was not feeling well and had sent for the night doctor. I then urged her to take her medication and eat something. I sat with her until the doctor arrived.

Line 21–25

It was myself who sent my son to the chemist and I gave him £5 for his fares. I dispute that she had suffered a violent attack by me or that I had been violent to her.

Line 27–37

I dispute searching through her handbag and stealing her keys. When she was in problems with the Council she would come to me and show me the letter. That was how I knew where she was.

I did not let myself into the flat. I went there and was let in by my son Anthony. He had a girl with him and they said they were waiting for a cousin of the girl. His name was Lee. He had gone to the shops. On Lee's arrival I could see they were up to no good and abusing the property so I told Lee and the girl to leave and my son Anthony went to see them off.

A few minutes later they returned, thinking I had gone and I told them to leave again and for Anthony to go to my house, and they did so. Because of this I decided to stay for a while to see whether they would return but I fell asleep for about one and half hours. I then left when I woke up.

I did not leave the next day as she claimed I left after one and half hours.

I was not waiting for her. I did not have any keys and told her to ask Anthony as he let me in. I was not violent. No police have ever questioned me about keys.

Statement of Anthony Jones

Dated 17th July 1999

Line 4–8

I did not assault his mother. These words were put into his mouth.

He was not present when I pushed my wife to the settee. The incident happened late on 23rd April 1999. I was not out celebrating, I went window shopping.

Line 12–13

I did say hello and gave them all my family friends greetings.

They were all there watching Sky TV and then went to their rooms because I wanted to watch the 10pm news as I always do.

Line 18–20

I dispute that I was pinning my wife down as I was standing in front of the single settee where I was previous sitting. I dispute having my hand around her neck. This is a blatant lie.

Line 20–22

If I had my back to him how could he see that I was strangling her.

I dispute that he had to pull me off because I saw them coming.

Line 23–30

I did not tell them "you should warn your mother, she is getting on my nerves".

All my wife did was to take her shoe off and throw it at me. I cannot comment on the marks around her neck as by then I was locked in the bedroom.

Line 35–40

My wife's eye was swollen because she was crying and getting herself worked up when I locked myself in the room.

I dispute that I have always beaten my wife. It is a lie that I have tried to strangle her 3–4 times before.

Line 41–45

I have always cared for my wife knowing she was diabetic.

Statement of Mr G.P. Who

Dated 20 August 1999

I cannot comment on this statement except to say when my wife does not take her medication she swells up.

Statement of PC Donald Dixon

Dated 28 August 1999

Line 5–8

He is saying I assaulted my wife as if he was there. He was not there and I dispute this.

Statement of PC Donald Dixon

Dated 27th September 1999

I have no comment on this statement.

Statement of Juliet Jones

Dated 16th October 1999

Line 5–9

I dispute telling her to withdraw the case and if I go to prison I will "Do her". I don't know where she got this from.

All I said to her concerning this case was that the police came to arrest me and made a case against me but I have written to the police saying that I did not want to say anything against her in public in keeping the promise I made to her throughout our married life.

Line 10–14

After the case nothing happened at Walworth Green Magistrates' Court. We went to my place and she followed me and my brother out at her will. I did not invite her along. No money was handed over at Walworth Green Magistrates' Court.

Line 15–18

When we got to the house I prepared a meal and we all ate. She and my brother drank a pint of beer even though she was not supposed to drink. After the meal I went to the kitchen and on my return she told me to thank my brother because he had given her £10 for her fare home. She continued to complain and accuse me of not giving her money of which I dispute.

I told her that I sent two cheques and misplaced the third one and that I had withdrawn cash. I then produced a cheque and cash and said that I had forgotten to give it to her because I was grieving. My brother then told her to take the money and stop complaining but she refused. My brother did not tell her to withdraw the case.

Statement of PC Donald Dixon

Dated 1st November 1999

I cannot comment on this as I have already dealt with my wife's statement.

Statement of PC Donald Dixon

Dated 18th October 1999

I have no comments on this statement.

Statement of PC Donald Dixon

Dated 7th November 1999

I have no comments.

Case Study B – Family/Injunction

File: Juliet Smith

Ref: VG/ Smith

Attendance Note

Date: 09/10/01

VG attending client in office. She resides at 35 Waylett Road Streatham London SW16 9AB.

DOB 23/02/62 Tel: 0208–769–3301 Mobile: 0865–321–123

Client stated she would like her partner to leave her home. She is not married to him and there are three children involved, one girl and two boys. Client stated she has custody of all three. She confirmed she had applied for Legal Aid before and her former solicitors are Useless & Co. Solicitors. She also confirmed that she has never applied for an injunction before.

She said that on Thursday 3rd October she was assaulted by her partner Romeo Jones and she had to call the police who came from New Park Police Station. She stated he has threatened to shoot her and accused her of having an affair. The threats were made in front of the children which resulted in her son having an asthma attack. She confirmed they have been together on and off for about 13 years.

The incident was reported to her doctor – Dr Heart Tel: 0208–769–9999. She also went to St. Peters Hospital two years ago when she was head-butted by her partner on her nose.

I completed Legal Aid forms and explained that I would try to get emergency Legal Aid.

VG telephoning Legal Aid Board to try and obtain emergency Legal Aid. This was refused on the basis that the incident took place on the 3rd October and we had to therefore apply for Legal Aid through the normal channels. Client confirmed that she would like her file with her former solicitors transferred to this office and signed authorisation to that effect.

ENGAGED 1hr

10/10/01

VG received telephone call from client. She confirmed that her boyfriend was moving out and requested that I still apply for Legal Aid in the normal way and if things work out then she would not proceed with the injunction.

11/10/01

VG attending client in office. She stated she had just been assaulted by her boyfriend when she went to see her son. She confirmed that she did not provoke him but he felt that she was "winding him up" by attending his address to see her son. She stated he accused her again of being unfaithful and threatened to shoot her and her lover. He punched her twice in her face.

Client reported matter to New Park Police Station. She also has an appointment to see her doctor.

File: J Smith

Ref: VG/Smith

Attendance Note

Dated: 18/10/01

VG telephoning client informing her that Legal Aid had been granted for her to take injunction proceedings. I also informed her that her file from her former solicitors had arrived.

21/10/01

VG/Smith

Juliet Smith
35 Waylett Road
Streatham
London
SW16 9AB

Dear Juliet,

Re: Injunction

Further to our recent telephone conversation I write to confirm that emergency legal aid has been granted for you to take injunction proceedings.

I also confirm that your file from your former solicitors has arrived at this office.

I would be grateful if you would telephone me to arrange a convenient appointment to discuss this matter and take your further instructions.

Yours sincerely

V. Good

File: J Smith

Ref: VG/Smith

Date: 21/10/01

Attendance Note

VG attending client in office taking instructions for affidavit.

ENGAGED 45mins

File: J. Smith

Date: 21/10/01

Attendance Note

VG drafting application for injunction.

ENGAGED 15 Mins

VG dictating affidavit in support and brief to counsel.

ENGAGED 1hr

File: J. Smith

Date: 23/10/01

Attendance Note

VG telephoning client arranging an appointment for Friday 28th October @ 11am to swear affidavit.

File: J. Smith

Date: 28/10/01

Attendance Note

VG receiving telephone call from client informing she will be a little late for the appointment today.

VG attending client in office discussing and making minor amendments to her affidavit. Client supplied a photograph of the Respondent which is now on file. I also gave client £5.00 to attend an independent solicitor to swear her affidavit.

ENGAGED 30 mins

File: J. Smith

Date: 28/10/01

Attendance Note

VG telephoning Process Server & Co. speaking to a lady by the name of Ann arranging for a Process Server to be on standby to attend and collect the papers for service.

VG attending Streatham County Court to issue injunction application. The clerk pointed out that as it was in the afternoon the issuing clerk was overwhelmed with work and in any event he would not issue the application until Monday. I therefore decided to take the application back to issue on Monday.

ENGAGED 45 mins

TRAVEL CLAIMED ELSEWHERE

VG telephoning client explaining that the application was not issued and as she was arranging to spend the weekend at her mother's I pointed out that there was no need for that as the papers would not be served over the weekend. I explained I would discuss the matter with her once the papers have been issued.

VG telephoning Process Server & Co. informing that the papers had not been issued and we will contact them on Monday.

TIME ENGAGED 15 mins

File: J. Smith

Date: 30/10/01

Attendance Note

VG attending Streatham County Court to collect issued injunction application lodged yesterday. The application was collected with a hearing date of 8th November 2001 at 10.30am

TRAVEL 1hr

ENGAGED 15 mins

FARES £2.50

VG telephoning client explaining that we now have a court date of 8th November. I explained I would confirm the hearing date in writing to her.

Date: 31/10/01

Ref: VG/Smith

Juliet Smith
35 Waylett Road
Streatham
London
SW16 9AB

Dear Juliet,

Re: Injunction at STREATHAM COUNTY COURT 76 Streatham High Road SW16
DATE OF HEARING: 8th November 2001 at 10am.

Further to our telephone conversation I write to confirm that your injunction application has been listed as above. I will be arranging for a barrister to represent you and will arrange for a representative from this firm to attend on that day.

I will also inform you when the papers are likely to be served on the Respondent in order for you to take the necessary precautions.

In the meantime should you have any queries please do not hesitate to contact me.

Yours sincerely

V. GOOD

VG/Smith

Date: 01/11/01

Process Server & Co.
50 High Street
Mitcham Surrey
CR4 3NB

Dear Sirs,

Re: Romeo Jones

We enclose injunction papers, together with a photograph of the above respondent, to be served in time for the hearing on 8th November 2001.

We should be grateful if you would telephone our client Juliet Smith on 0208–769–3301 or 0865–321–123 once the papers have been served.

We look forward to hearing from you.

Yours faithfully

V. Good & Co. Solicitors

File: J. Smith

Date: 01/11/01

Attendance Note

VG telephoning client informing that I will be instructing the Process Server to collect the documents to be served either on Saturday or sometime next week.

VG attending Process Server in office explaining the whereabouts of the respondent and giving client details, including papers to be served.

ENGAGED 10 mins

VG telephoning client informing that the injunction papers are now with the Process Server to be served. He will telephone her to discuss the respondent's movements.

VG/Smith

Date: 01/11/01

The Clerk to
Michael Hopeton
3 Counsel's Chambers
Temple
London
EC4Y 7JA

Dear Sir,

RE: JULIET SMITH
INJUNCTION APPLICATION AT STREATHAM COUNTY COURT
DATE OF HEARING: 8th NOVEMBER 2001 @ 10am

Please find enclosed brief for placing before Counsel.

Yours faithfully

V. Good & Co.

File: J Smith

Date: 5/11/01

Attendance Note

VG telephoning Process Server speaking to a lady by the name of Ann regarding the serving of the injunction papers. I was told that the Process Server had been to the premises on three occasions without success and made an appointment to attend tonight at 9pm. She said it was confirmed that he does reside there but is being elusive. They will get back to us as soon as the papers are served.

File: J Smith

Date: 06/11/01

Attendance Note

VG receiving telephone call from Process Server & Co. informing that the agent had attended the premises last night by appointment and was told by the lady that he does not live there. As a result the process server will have to do an affidavit of attempted service.

VG/Smith

Date: 07/11/01

The List Office
Streatham County Court
76 Streatham High Road
London
SW16

FAX 0208–769–5498

Dear Sirs,

RE: SMITH V JONES – CASE NO: 96DV1001 – DOH 8/11/01 @ 10.30 AM

The Respondent has been avoiding service of the injunction papers in this matter and the papers have therefore not been served in time for the above hearing.

We enclose a Notice of Application to seek an order at the hearing for substituted service and should be grateful if you would issue this to be heard at the same time.

Yours faithfully

V. Good & Co.

File: J Smith

Date: 07/11/01

Attendance Note

VG telephoning Streatham County Court list office who confirmed they had received our letter informing them that at the hearing listed for the injunction tomorrow we will be applying for an order for substituted service. It was confirmed the letter will be placed on file.

VG drafting additional affidavit.

ENGAGED 30 mins

VG telephoning Process Server to confirm whether or not the agent might be able to attend court tomorrow morning. I was told the agent would be attending our office today in any event to deliver the affidavit of attempted service but she would check and phone me back.

VG receiving telephone call from Process Server & Co. who confirmed that the agent would be able to attend court if necessary. I explained I would confirm once I have spoken to counsel.

VG telephoning counsel Michael Hopeton speaking to the clerk who said that he was not in the office and would arrange for him to phone me back.

VG telephoning client reading additional draft affidavit to her, amending same. I reminded her to be at court for 10am tomorrow morning.

ENGAGED 10 mins

File: J Smith

VG/Smith

Date: 8/11/01

VG attending Streatham County Court on injunction application.

On arrival both client and counsel were already present and I duly handed counsel the affidavit of service together with client's second affidavit.

Counsel confirmed that client had stated that on Saturday the respondent had threatened her again and was seen to be hanging around her property by a neighbour. Counsel took further instructions from client and we went and swore her second affidavit.

In view of the problem of serving the documents and client's instructions that the respondent was seen hanging around her property Counsel requested that I drafted a 3rd affidavit. This affidavit was not completed as we were called into court.

In court Counsel pointed out the difficulties and requested either that the matter be dealt with ex parte (without notice) or that an order for substituted service be granted and invited His Honour to grant the injunction to be served at the same time.

Having read the papers His Honour granted the order as requested for six months with a Power of Arrest attached to numbers 1, 3 and 4 which is to last for three months.

His Honour also ordered that the order was made ex parte (without notice) but deemed to be served if delivered to the sister-in-law's house at 25 Mitcham Road SW12 by noon on the 9th November 2001.

The respondent has liberty to vary the order on giving two days notice.

Outside court we were asked to draft the order which then had to be submitted back to the judge for his signature.

COURT:	STREATHAM COUNTY
COURT NUMBER:	2
JUDGE:	HH JUDGE VINCENT
COUNSEL:	MICHAEL HOPETON
TRAVEL:	2 hrs
CONFERENCE:	30 mins
WAITING:	15 mins
HEARING:	15 mins
ATTENDANCE:	30 mins
MILEAGE:	20
PARKING:	£3.00

VG/Smith

Date: 08/11/01

Mr Romeo Jones
25 Mitcham Road
London
SW12 5AD

Dear Sir,

RE: JULIET SMITH OF 35 WAYLETT ROAD LONDON SW16

We enclose by way of service on you, an injunction order together with POWER OF ARREST granted at Streatham County Court on 08/11/01.

You will note you are forbidden from:

1. Using or threatening to use violence against the Applicant (Miss Smith).

2. Molesting, pestering or otherwise interfering with the Applicant (Miss Smith).

3. Contacting Miss Smith the Applicant, directly or indirectly save through your solicitors and for the purpose of contact only.

4. Coming within 100 yards of 35 Waylett Road SW16.

You will also note a POWER OF ARREST has been attached to this order which means you can be arrested and imprisoned in the event that you breach this injunction order.

If you have any queries we suggest you seek independent legal advice.

Yours faithfully

V. Good & Co.

VG/Smith

Date: 08/11/01

New Park Police Station
10 New Park Road
London
SW2 2AY

Dear Sirs,

RE: JULIET SMITH OF 35 WAYLETT ROAD LONDON SW16 9AB

We enclose an order for injunction together with POWER OF ARREST granted at Streatham County Court on 8/11/01 to be registered at your station.

Yours faithfully

V. Good & Co.

IN THE STREATHAM COUNTY COURT   **NO: 96DV1001**

LEGAL AID

BETWEEN:

<table>
<tr><td align="center">JULIET SMITH</td><td align="right">APPLICANT</td></tr>
<tr><td align="center">— AND —</td><td></td></tr>
<tr><td align="center">ROMEO JONES</td><td align="right">RESPONDENT</td></tr>
</table>

BRIEF TO COUNSEL

Counsel has herewith:

1. Application for injunction
2. Affidavit in support
3. Copy legal aid certificate

Counsel is instructed on behalf of the Applicant Juliet Smith, born 23/2/62 who resides at 35 Waylett Road Streatham London SW16 9AB.

For full details Counsel is referred to the Applicant's affidavit herewith. However, Counsel should note that both these parties were before the court in proceedings under s.8 of the Children Act 1989. Both parties however reconciled and the matter was withdrawn.

Counsel will note from the injunction application that a request has been made for the return of Robert's passport which the Respondent took when he was asked to leave the home. The applicant is concerned that the Respondent might be planning to return to America and could take Robert with him. As far as the instructing solicitors are aware, there is no Prohibitive Steps Order in force under the old proceedings, which were withdrawn in any event.

Counsel will note that the Applicant is very concerned that the Respondent will carry out further attacks when he finds out about these proceedings and at the time of dictating these instructions was considering applying ex parte.

Counsel will also note that the last assault was on the 11th October and on each of the last two occasions the Applicant suffered two black eyes and bruising to the face. For this reason counsel is requested to apply for a Power of Arrest to be attached to the injunction.

Counsel is instructed to attend and represent the Applicant on the injunction application and should not hesitate to contact Mr Victor Good of instructing solicitors should there be any queries.

Counsel is instructed accordingly.

V. Good & Co.
22/10/01

DEPONENT:
NO OF AFFIDAVIT:
DATE SWORN:
DATE FILED:

In the Streatham County Court   No: 96DV1001

Between:

Juliet Smith	**Applicant**
[and]	
Romeo Jones	**Respondent**

Second Affidavit of the Applicant

V. Good & Co.
18, Miranda Road
Streatham
London
SW16 7AG
TEL: 0208–769–9001
FAX:0208–769–9002
DX: 3772 Streatham
REF: VG/S.547/01

DEPONENT:
NO OF AFFIDAVIT:
DATE SWORN:
DATE FILED:

IN THE STREATHAM COUNTY COURT   No: 96DV1001

BETWEEN:

JULIET SMITH	**APPLICANT**
[AND]	
ROMEO JONES	**RESPONDENT**

FIRST AFFIDAVIT OF THE APPLICANT

V. Good & Co.
18, Miranda Road
Streatham
London
SW16 7AG
TEL: 0208–769–9001
FAX:0208–769–9002
DX: 3772 Streatham
REF: VG/S.547/01

DEPONENT:
NO OF AFFIDAVIT:
DATE SWORN:
DATE FILED:

IN THE STREATHAM COUNTY COURT   No: 96DV1001

BETWEEN:

JULIET SMITH   APPLICANT

[AND]

ROMEO JONES   RESPONDENT

AFFIDAVIT OF ATTEMPTED SERVICE

I, DAVID BROWN, of Process Servers & Co. of 50 High Street, Mitcham, Surrey CR4 3NB, process server being over the age of sixteen years and acting under the instructions of V. Good & Co. Solicitors of 18 Miranda Road, Streatham, SW16 7AG acting on behalf of the Applicant in this matter JULIET SMITH, make oath and say as follows:

1. That being directed to effect personal service of an Application for an Injunction bearing the date the 25th October 2001 with an Affidavit in support for hearing on Friday 8th November 2001 at 10.30am, I did on Friday the 1st November 2001 at 5.20pm attend at 25 Mitcham Road, SW12 an address supplied to me by my instructing solicitors. On my attendance there at 5.20pm I was unable to obtain any answer whatsoever and I made enquiries in the vicinity from neighbours but nobody could assist. A call was made later that evening and still there was no one at the address.

2. On Saturday 2nd November 2001 at 6.30pm I again attended at the address and on this occasion the door was answered by an adult female in her late twenties to early thirties and when I asked to speak with Romeo Jones she said "No". I then said to her what about Monday, again she said "No" and slammed the door in my face. At this time the person

had no idea of the purpose of my call and I had only attended at the address and asked for the person, Romeo Jones.

3. On Monday 4th November 2001 I made an early morning call at the address. I had someone else call at the door and there was no reply. I then placed the premises under observation from 8.30am but I saw no one answering the description of any male whatsoever come out of the address. After spending over an hour at the address I then drew up a letter of appointment for Tuesday 6th November for 9.00pm.

4. On Tuesday 6th November 2001 at 9.00pm I duly attended at the address in accordance with my letter of appointment. The door was answered by the woman I met previously and on this occasion she spoke more to me. She stated that she had spoken to the Applicant the same day over the telephone and that (the Applicant) had explained to her about the injunction. She the Applicant, had given her solicitors the address of 25 Mitcham Road London SW12 as a care of address as she had no other address for the respondent. The adult female at the address claimed that the subject did not reside there and that she had not seen him for over a week and that she was most upset that her address was being used. She then stated that she would take my telephone number and that if she saw him or spoke to him she would pass this on and ask him to telephone. I have not received any telephone calls whatsoever since I gave the woman at 25 Mitcham Road, SW12 my telephone number.

5. As a result of the enquires I have made I am of the opinion that there is little likelihood of me meeting personally with the Respondent Romeo Jones at the address of 25 Mitcham Road, London, SW12 and that I will not be able to effect personal service of the said Application upon him.

6. That I have attempted to meet personally with the Respondent Romeo Jones on numerous occasions but have been unable to do so therefore I was unable to serve him personally with the aforementioned documents in time for the hearing on the 8th November 2001.

SWORN BY

THIS   **DAY OF**   **2001**

AT

BEFORE ME,

DEPONENT:
NO OF AFFIDAVIT:
DATE SWORN:
DATE FILED:

IN THE STREATHAM COUNTY COURT   No: 96DV1001

BETWEEN:

<table>
<tr><td>JULIET SMITH</td><td>APPLICANT</td></tr>
<tr><td>[AND]</td><td></td></tr>
<tr><td>ROMEO JONES</td><td>RESPONDENT</td></tr>
</table>

AFFIDAVIT OF ATTEMPTED SERVICE

Process Server & Co.
50 High Street
Mitcham
Surrey
CR4 3NB
TEL: 0208–680–5559
FAX: 208–680–1528

DEPONENT:
NO OF AFFIDAVIT:
DATE SWORN:
DATE FILED:

IN THE STREATHAM COUNTY COURT   No: 96DV1001

BETWEEN:

JULIET SMITH   APPLICANT

[AND]

ROMEO JONES   RESPONDENT

SECOND AFFIDAVIT OF THE APPLICANT

**I, JULIET SMITH of 35 Waylett Road Streatham London SW16 9AB
MAKE OATH AND SAY as follows:**

1. I am the Applicant herein and I make this second affidavit in support of
    my application for substituted service on the Respondent.

2. The Respondent used to live at 28, Albert Square London SW4 and has
    since moved to an address off Brixton Road SW9 the address of which I
    do not know.

3. The c/o address namely 25 Mitcham Road SW12 belongs to his sister-in-
    law. The Respondent has contact with our son Robert Smith every
    weekend from Friday 7pm to Sunday 8pm at this address. This is an
    informal arrangement between his sister-in-law and myself to avoid any
    contact between myself and the Respondent. I believe he does visit and
    sometimes sleeps there in the week.

4. I have no doubt that any papers delivered to 25 Mitcham Road SW12
    would come to the attention of the Respondent.

5. As mentioned in my previous affidavit, these assaults were reported to
    the police and has been dealt with by WPC KAREN WILKINSON of the

Domestic Violence Unit at New Park Police Station. The crime reference number is MM999/96/JS.

6. My home beat officer PC Allen is also investigating the matter. I understand the police are also having difficulty tracing him.

7. In these circumstances I ask this Honourable Court to grant the order for substituted service.

SWORN BY

THIS   DAY OF   2001

AT

BEFORE ME,

DEPONENT:
NO OF AFFIDAVIT:
DATE SWORN:
DATE FILED:

IN THE STREATHAM COUNTY COURT   **No: 96DV1001**

BETWEEN:

JULIET SMITH   **APPLICANT**

[AND]

ROMEO JONES   **RESPONDENT**

FIRST AFFIDAVIT OF THE APPLICANT

I, JULIET SMITH of 35 Waylett Road Streatham London SW16 9AB MAKE OATH AND SAY as follows:

1. I am the Applicant herein and I met the Respondent 13 years ago. We started to cohabit soon thereafter. There are two children of this relationship namely Sydney Smith born 28/4/98 and Robert Smith born 20/3/91.

2. The Respondent started verbally abusing me soon after Robert was born and turned to physical violence sometime thereafter in 1986. On this occasion the Respondent punched me in the jaw and I had to attend Queen's College Hospital. I did not report this to the police.

3. Although the verbal abuse continued, the next occasion when the Respondent physically assaulted me was after Sydney was born in 1993, when the Respondent head-butted me on my nose. As a result I had to attend St. Peter's Hospital in Balham where I obtained stitches. Again I did not report this to the police.

4. The Respondent continued to be verbally abusive and threatened to assault me and for peace and quiet I kept my mouth shut and avoided answering him back. However, on the odd occasions when I said

something in reply he would again threatened me and make his hand in the form of a gun and point it at me making the gestures of shooting me.

5. The Respondent went to America in April 2001 for four months and on his return he accused me of having an affair with a male friend of mine. As a result I told him that the relationship was over as I could not take his abuse anymore. He did not like that and threatened to shoot me.

6. On the 2/10/01 I went out with a friend and left the Respondent to babysit. I arrived home in the early morning only to be verbally abused by the Respondent, calling me all sorts of names and telling me to go back to where I had come from. He again threatened to shoot me or else. He again formed his fingers into the shape of a gun and threatened to shoot me and my so-called lover.

7. As a result of this Robert woke up and the Respondent continued to verbally abuse me in front of him. I went upstairs and he followed me and came up close as if he was going to hit me. In fear I pushed him and he punched me three times in my face. In panic I started to hit him back and his T-shirt got ripped in the process. Robert started crying and shouting. The police were called and asked the Respondent to leave the premises which he did.

8. On the 11/10/01 I went to see my son who was having contact with the Respondent and again without provocation the Respondent verbally abused and punched me twice in my face in front of my son and other witnesses. Again he threatened to shoot me and my so-called lover. I reported this to the police at New Park Police Station.

9. The Respondent does not live at the address where he has contact with my son and I have no idea where he is living. I know from his circles of friends and associates that the Respondent has the means and access of obtaining a gun. I am in fear that once he finds out that the police are taking this matter seriously and that he is being investigated he will go berserk and assault me again without the protection of the court.

10. In these circumstances I ask this Honourable Court to grant me the court's protection.

SWORN BY

THIS   DAY OF   2001

AT

BEFORE ME,

APPENDIX 2
SPECIMEN DOCUMENTS

Specimen Case Summary

DATE: 20/2/00

CLIENT: ROMEO JONES

COURT: STREATHAM CROWN COURT (SCC)

COURT NO: 5

JUDGE: D.J. EVANS

COUNSEL: MICHAEL HOPETON

Case Summary

CW attending (SCC) when the following **ORDER** was made and **DIRECTIONS** given:

Crown to serve the Defence with the following within 14 days:

1. Interview transcript
2. CAD messages
3. Police Doctor's report
4. Photographs
5. Confirmation as to whether victim has ever received psychiatric treatment

Client pleaded not guilty to all charges. The witness intimidation charge was dropped. Matter to enter warned list for period commencing 3/4/00.

FULL DETAILED ATTENDANCE NOTE TO FOLLOW

NAME OF CLERK Christopher Wilson

Attendance Note

Date: _____ 20th FEBRUARY 2000 _____

Ref/Sols: _____ DP/V. Good & Co. Solicitors, _____ 99 Valley Field Road, Streatham London SW16 DX 3210 Streatham _____

Name of Client: _____ ROMEO JONES _____

Times

Travel:	*From:*	8.40	*To:*	10.10	*Total:*	
	From:	13.00	*To:*	14.40	*Total:*	
Waiting:	*From:*	10.10	*To:*	10.25	*Total:*	
	From:	10.45	*To:*	11.40	*Total:*	
		11.55		12.30	*Total:*	
Attendance/	*From:*	10.25	*To:*	10.45	*Total:*	
Conference	*From:*	11.40	*To:*	11.55	*Total:*	
		12.50		13.00	*Total:*	
Hearing:	*From:*	12.30	*To:*	12.50	*Total:*	
	From:		*To:*		*Total:*	

Court: Streatham Crown Court (SCC)

Court No: 5

Judge: H.H.J. Evans

Counsel: Michael Hopeton

Mileage:

Fares: £3.00

Phone: x 2 (40p)

Out of pocket expenses:

Nature of work done: CW attending SCC on Plea and Directions hearing

PLEASE SEE ATTACHED

CW attending Streatham Crown Court on Pleas and Directions hearing in the case of Romeo Jones. I arrived at Court at 10.10. Counsel was not present. I met Counsel and client at reception at 10.25. Client was on conditional bail.

We then went into conference where Counsel went through the victim's statement with regards to the witness intimidation and took further instructions. Counsel advised client that the evidence against him for the intimidation charge was very weak due to the presence of a witness. Counsel clarified the circumstances which lead to that charge.

With regards to the assault charge Counsel informed client that the prosecution had sufficient evidence to present a case to the jury. Counsel explained the difficulty with the marks around his wife's neck which client states was self-inflicted. Counsel explained without an expert report confirming that someone with his wife' medical condition sometimes causes injury to themselves, it will be difficult trying to convince the jury that the wounds were self-inflicted and the client may well be found guilty.

Client confirmed that he was not guilty and wished to defend the case.

Counsel then left to speak to the prosecutor and upon his return he confirmed that the Crown were going to drop the intimidation charge.

Counsel then clarified the documents which the CPS has so far failed to disclose to us in order to bring these to the attention of the judge.

The hearing commenced at 12.30 before HHJ Evans when client was arraigned to which client pleaded not guilty to all charges. The prosecutor then formerly withdrew the witness intimidation charge. The prosecutor agreed to provide instructing solicitors with the documents and information requested within 14 days. HH then ordered that the matter be entered on the warned list for the week commencing 3rd April 2000.

Counsel then addressed HH on client's bail and requested that client be bailed as before which was granted. The hearing ended.

Outside court Counsel had a final conference with client and explained what would happen after today. Counsel requested we have a conference closer to the trial and once we have received the documents from the CPS. Counsel advised that we list the matter for mention if we do not receive the documents within the 14 days as ordered. Conference ended.

I left court at 13.00 hours, telephoned V Good & Co. Solicitors to let them know the outcome of the hearing and then travelled to their offices in order to return the files to them.

NAME OF CLERK _____

Attendance Note

Date: _____

Ref/Sols: _____

_____

Name of Client: _____

Times

Travel: From: _____   To: _____   Total: _____
                From: _____   To: _____   Total: _____

Waiting: From: _____   To: _____   Total: _____
                From: _____   To: _____   Total: _____

Attendance/   From: _____   To: _____   Total: _____
Conference   From: _____   To: _____   Total: _____

Hearing: From: _____   To: _____   Total: _____
                From: _____   To: _____   Total: _____

Court:

Court No:

Judge:

Counsel:

Mileage:

Fares:

Phone:

Out of pocket expenses:

Nature of work done: _____

_____

_____

_____.

Specimen Invoice

Date: _____

Name of Clerk: _____

Address: _____

_____

_____

Date of attendance: _____

Solicitors: _____

Address: _____

_____

_____

Client: _____

Nature of work done: _____

_____

_____

	Times			**Details**	**Amount**
Travel:	From:	To:	Total:		
	From:	To:	Total:	Fixed Fee	£
Waiting:	From:	To:	Total:		
	From:	To:	Total:	Phone	£
Attendance/	From:	To:	Total:	Total milage	
Conference	From:	To:	Total:	@_____ p	£
Hearing:	From:	To:	Total:		
	From:	To:	Total:	Fares	£
				Out of pocket expenses	£
					_____
				TOTAL DUE	£
					_____

Cheque made payable to _____

Specimen Letter

Mr Simon Smith
46 Queens Parade
London
SW13 2PR

TEL: 020 8 936 4321
MOBILE: 0695 772 098

DATE:

Mr Victor Good
V. GOOD & CO
18, Miranda Road
Streatham
LONDON
SW16 7AG

Dear Sir,

Re Freelance Clerking Services

This letter is to enquire whether you use freelance Paralegal/Outdoor Clerks and to advertise my services and availability to work as and when required.

I have experience of:

– Assisting Barristers at court in Criminal/Family/Civil proceedings
– Attending on conferences
– Taking witness Statements
– Presenting District Judges Applications
– Other

I would be grateful if you would place my name on the list of Clerks that you use from time to time.

If necessary, I am willing to provide a week unpaid voluntary work in order for you to assess me prior to using me on a regular basis.

I hope you will find this letter and my services of interest and look forward to hearing from you.

Yours Faithfully

Simon Smith
(Freelance Paralegal Clerk)

APPENDIX 3
USEFUL INFORMATION

Map of WC2 area

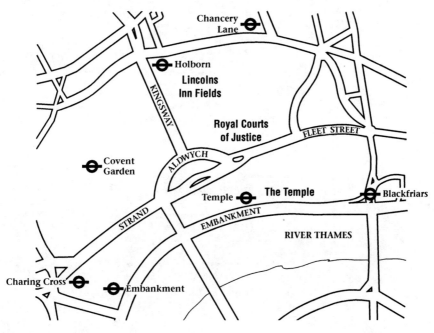

Example of General Court Room Setting

JUDGE	

WITNESS BOX

CLERK	STENOGRAPHER

USHER

PROSECUTION/ PLAINTIFF BARRISTER/ ADVOCATE	DEFENCE BARRISTER/ ADVOCATE

CROWN/ PLAINTIFF/ SOLICITORS/ CLERK/CLIENT	DEFENCE SOLICITORS/ CLERK/CLIENT

PUBLIC GALLERY

PUBLIC GALLERY

DEFENDANT/ CLIENT IN DOCK

J U R Y   J U R Y

KEY:

(1) PROSECUTION CROWN CLERK
     DEFENDANT/CLIENT IN DOCK}   APPLY TO CRIMINAL CASES ONLY

(2) ALL OTHER PARTIES}   APPLY TO CRIMINAL/OTHER CASES

(3) POSITION OF PUBLIC GALLERY
     & DEFENDANT IN DOCK VARIES

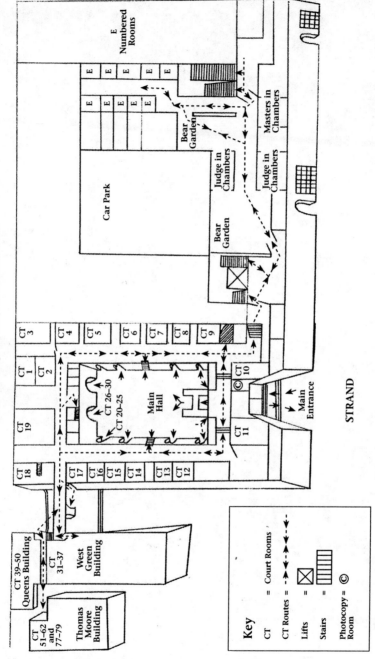

Map of Royal Courts of Justice

APPENDIX 4
LIST OF COUNTY AND CROWN COURTS, POLICE CONTACT TELEPHONE NUMBERS, PRISONS AND EMPLOYMENT TRIBUNALS

List of County/Crown Courts in England and Wales

All Courts are listed in Alphabetical Order

County Courts

Aberystwyth County Court
Eddleston House,
Queens Road, Aberystwyth
Tel: 01970 617 597
Fax: 01970 625 985

Aberdare County Court
Crown Building,
Green St, Aberdare,
Mid-Glamorgan CF44 7DW
Tel: 01685 874 779
Fax: 01685 883 413

Accrington County Court
Bradshawgate House,
1 Oak St, Accrington, Lancs BB5 1EQ
Tel: 01254 398 173/237 490
Fax: 01254 393 869

Aldershot & Farnham County Court
78/82 Victoria Road,
Aldershot, Hants GU11 1SS
Tel: 01252 21639/331607/8
Fax: 01252 345705

Alnwick County Court
Roxburgh House,
Greenbatt, Alnwick,
Northumberland NE66 1TJ
Tel: 01665 602642

Altrincham County Court
16 Grafton Street,
Altrincham, Cheshire WA14 1DX
Tel: 0161 9281444/9411674
Fax: 0161 9268374

Ammanford County Court
48 College Street,
Ammanford, Dyfed SA18 3AF
Tel: 01269 592563
Fax: 01269 591106

Andover County Court
Chantry House, Chantry Way,
Andover, Hants SP10 1NB
Tel: 01264 366622
Fax: 01264 338983

Ashford County Court
Orchard House, Tannery Lane,
Station Road, Ashford, Kent TN23 1PL
Tel: 01233 632464
Fax: 01233 612786

Aylesbury County Court
Second floor, Heron House,
Buckingham Street, Aylesbury, Bucks
HP20 2NQ
Tel: 01296 397498
Fax: 01296 397363

Banbury County Court
35 Parsons Street, Banbury,
Oxon OX16 8BW
Tel: 01295 265799
Fax: 01295 277025

Barnet County Court
St Mary's Court, Regents Park Road,
Finchley Central, London N3 1BQ
Tel: 0208 343 4272
Fax: 0208 343 1324

Barnsley County Court
12 Regent St, Barnsley,
S. Yorks S70 2EW
Tel: 01226 203471
Fax: 01226 779126

Barnstaple County Court
The Law Court, Civic Centre,
North Walk, Barnstable, Devon
EX31 1DY
Tel: 01271 72252
Fax: 01271 22968

Barrow-in-Furness County Court
Government Buildings,
Michaelson Road, Barrow-in-Furness,
Cumbria LA14 2EZ
Tel: 01229 820046/827150
Fax: 01229 430039

Basingstoke County Court
3rd Floor, Grosvenor House,
Basing View, Basingstoke RG12 1BR
Tel: 01256 22754/50525
Fax: 01256 57131

Bath County Court
3rd and 4th Floor, Cambridge House,
Henry Street, Bath BA1 1D
Tel: 01225 310282
Fax: 01225 480915

Bedford County Court
29 Goldington Road, Bedford
MK40 3NN
Tel: 01234 359322
Fax: 01234 327431

Berwick upon Tweed County Court
Norham House, 15 Walkergate,
Berwick-upon-Tweed TD15 1DS
Tel: 01289 305053

Birkenhead County Court
76 Hamilton St, Birkenhead,
Merseyside L41 5EN
Tel: 0151 6478826/6479676
Fax: 0151 6473501

Birmingham County Court
33 Bull Street, Birmingham B4 7LU
Tel: 0121 6813000
Fax: 0121 6813001

Bishop Auckland County Court
Saddler House, Saddler Street,
Bishop Auckland, Co Durham
DL14 7HF
Tel: 01388 602423
Fax: 01388 606651

Bishop's Stortford County Court
27 Northgate End, Bishop's Stortford,
Herts CM23 2EZ
Tel: 01279 654445
Fax: 01279 758783

Blackburn County Court
64 Victoria St, Blackburn, Lancs BB1 6DJ
Tel: 01254 680640/680654
Fax: 01254 692712

Blackpool County Court
The Law Courts, Chapel Street,
Blackpool, Lancs FY1 5RJ
Tel: 01253 293178/9
Fax: 01253 295255

Blackwood County Court
County Court Office, Blackwood Rd,
Blackwood, Gwent NP2 2XB
Tel: 01495 223197
Fax: 01495 220289

Blyth County Court
73 Bridge Street, Blyth,
Northumberland NE24 2AL
Tel: 01670 352133

Bodmin County Court
(1) Cockswell House, Market St,
    Bodmin, Cornwall PL31 2JJ
    Tel: 01208 73735/74224
    Fax: 01208 77255
(2) Laity House, Liskeard, Cornwall
    Caller office County Court only
    Tel: 01579 42114

Bolton Combined Court Centre
The Law Courts, Blackhorse St,
Bolton, Lancs BL1 1SU
Tel: 01204 3392881
Fax: 01204 363204

Boston County Court
Crown Buildings, Lincoln Lane,
Boston, Lancs PE21 8SG
Tel: 01205 366080
Fax: 01205 311692

Bournemouth Combined Court Centre
Old Buildings, Law Courts, Stafford Road,
Bournemouth, Dorset BH1 1PN
Tel: 01202 553701
Fax: 01202 290819

Bow County Court
96 Romford Road, Stratford,
London E15 4EG
Tel: 0181 5553421
Fax: 0181 5198149

Bradford County Court
Exchange Square, Drake Street,
Bradford, W. Yorks BD1 1JA
Tel: 01274 840274
Fax: 01274 840275

Braintree County Court
70 Coggeshall Rd, Braintree,
Essex CM7 6DQ
Tel: 01376 551661
Fax: 01376 346200

Brecknock County Court
International Store Buildings,
32 High St, Superior, Brecon, Powys
LD3 7AN
Tel: 01874 622671
Fax: 01874 611607

Brentford County Court
Alexandra Road, Brentford,
Middlesex TW8 0JJ
Tel: 0181 5603424/5/6
Fax: 0181 5682401

Bridgend County Court
Crown Buildings, Angel Street,
Bridgend, Mid Glamorgan CF31 4AS
Tel: 01656 768881
Fax: 01656 647124

Bridgwater County Court
Court House, Queen St,
Bridgwater, Somerset TA6 8AP
Tel: 01278 422180
Fax: 01278 446337

Bridlington County Court
19–20 Queen St, Bridlington,
N Humberside YO15 2SH
Tel: 01262 606030
Fax: 01262 401663

Brighton County Court
William Street, Brighton BN2 2LG
Tel: 01273 674421
Fax: 01273 602138

Bristol County Court
Greyfriars, Lewins Mead,
Bristol BSI 2NR
Tel: 0117 9294414
Fax: 0117 9250912

Bromley County Court
Court House, College Road,
Bromley Kent BR1 3PX
Tel: 0181 4649727
Fax: 0181 3139624

Burnley Combined Court Centre
The Law Courts, PO Box 30,
Hammerton Street, Burnley BB11 1XD
Tel: 01282 416899
Fax: 01282 414911

Burton-upon-Trent County Court
165 Station Street, Burton-upon-Trent,
Staffs DE14 1BP
Tel: 01283 568241/541277
Fax: 01283 517245

Bury County Court
Tenterden Street, Bury, Lancs BL9 OHU
Tel: 0161 7641344/9201
Fax: 0161 7641344

Bury St Edmunds County Court
Triton House, St Andrews Street North,
Bury St Edmunds, Suffolk IP33 1TR
Tel: 01284 753254
Fax: 01284 702687

Buxton County Court
1–3 Hardwick Street, Buxton,
Derby SK17 6DH
Tel: 01298 23734/71298
Fax: 01298 73281

Caernarfon County Court
Llanberis Road, Caernarfon,
Gwynedd LL55 2DF
Tel: 01286 678911
Fax: 01286 6788965

Caerphilly County Court
Crown Buildings, Claude Road
Entrance, Denscombe Estate, Caerphilly,
Mid Glam CF8 2WY
Tel: 01222 867616
Fax: 01222 861791

Camborne & Redruth County Court
Josiah Thomas Memorial Hall,
Fore Street, Camborne TR14 8AY
Tel: 01209 715585/6
Fax: 01209 715075

Cambridge County Court,
72–80 Hill Road, Cambridge CB2 1LA
Tel: 01223 354 416
Fax: 01223 324 775

Canterbury Combined Centre
The Law Courts, Chaucer Road,
Canterbury, Kent CT1 1ZA
Tel: 01227 819200
Fax: 01227 819329

Cardiff County Court
PO Box 64, 2 Park Street,
Cardiff, South Glamorgan CF1 1ET
Tel: 01222 376400
Fax: 01222 376469

Carlisle County Court (Combined)
Courts of Justice, Earl Street,
Carlisle, Cumbria CA1 1DJ
Tel: 01238 20619
Fax: 01238 590588

Carmarthen County Court
The Old Vicarage,
Picton Terrace Carmarthen SA31 1BJ
Tel: 01267 236598
Fax: 01267 221844

Central London County Court
13–14 Park Crescent, London W1N 3PD
Tel: 0207 9175000
Fax: 0207 9175014

Chelmsford County Court
London House, New London Road,
Chelmsford, Essex CM2 0QR
Tel: 01245 264670/281386
Fax: 01245 496523

Cheltenam County Court
The Court House, County Court Road,
Cheltenham, Glos GL50 1HB
Tel: 01242 519983
Fax: 01242 252741

Chepstow County Court
Station Road, Chepstow, Gwent
NP6 5YD
Tel: 01291 622097
Fax: 01291 627363

Chester County Court
1st floor, Centurion House,
77 Northgate Street, Chester CH1 2HB
Tel: 01244 312245
Fax: 01244 315635

Chesterfield County Court
49 Church Way, Chesterfield,
Derbys S40 1SG
Tel: 01246 501200
Fax: 01246 501220

Chichester Combined Courts
Southgate, Chichester, Sussex PO19 1SX
Tel: 01243 786151
Fax: 01243 533756

Chorley County Court
59 St Thomas's Road, Chorley PR7 1JE
Tel: 012572 62778
Fax: 012572 32843

Clerkenwell County Court
33 DuncanTerrace, Islington,
London N1 8AN
Tel: 0207 359 7347/9
Fax: 0207 354 1166

Colchester County Court
Falkland House, 25 Southway,
Colchester CO3 3EG
Tel: 01206 572743
Fax: 01206 369610

Consett County Court
Victoria Road, Consett,
Co. Durham DH8 5AU
Tel: 01207 502854
Fax: 01207 582626

Conwy and Colwyn County Court
49 Conwy Rd, Colwyn Bay,
Clwyd LL29 7AW
Tel: 01492 530807
Fax: 01492 533591

Corby County Court
52 Elizabeth Street, Corby,
Northants NN17 1PQ
Tel: 01536 202887
Fax: 01536 403395

Coventry Combined Court Centre
140 Much Park Street, Coventry,
W. Mids CV1 1SN
Tel: 01203 536166
Fax: 01203 520443

Crewe County Court
The Law Courts, Civic Centre,
Crewe, Cheshire CW1 2DP
Tel: 01270 212255/212693
Fax: 01270 216344

Croydon Combined Court Centre
The Law Centre, Altyre Road,
Croydon CR9 5AB
Tel: 0208 681 2533
Fax: 0208 760 0432

Darlington County Court
4 Conscliffe Road, Darlington,
Co. Durham DL3 7RG
Tel: 01325 463224
Fax: 01325 362829

Datford County Court
Court House, Home Gardens,
Dartford, Kent DA1 1DX
Tel: 01322 223396
Fax: 01322 270902

Derby Combined Court Centre
Morledge, Derby DE1 2XE
Tel: 01332 622600
Fax: 01332 622543

Dewsbury County Court
Combined Court House, Eightlands
Road, Dewsbury, W. Yorks HF13 2PE
Tel: 01924 465860/466135
Fax: 01924 456419

Doncaster County Court
74 Waterdale, Doncaster,
S. Yorks DN1 3BT
Tel: 01302 323733/365400
Fax: 01302 768090

Dudley County Court
61 The Broadway, Dudley,
W. Mids DY1 3EF
Tel: 01384 236321
Fax: 01384 257579

Durham County Court
Hallgarth Street, Durham DH1 3RG
Tel: 0191 3865941
Fax: 0191 3861328

Eastbourne County Court
4 The Avenue, Eastbourne BN21 3SZ
Tel: 01323 735195
Fax: 01323 638829

Edmonton County Court
Court House, 59 Fore Street,
Upper Edmonton N18 2TN
Tel: 0208 807 1666/7 or 0208 884 7755
Fax: 0208 8030564

Epsom County Court
The Parade, Epsom, Surrey KT18 5DN
Tel: 01372 721801
Fax: 01372 726588

Evesham County Court
1st Floor, 87 High Street, Evesham,
Worcs WR11 4EE
Tel: 01386 442287
Fax: 01386 49203

Exeter Combined Court Centre
The Castle, Exeter, Devon EX4 3PS
Tel: 01392 210655
Fax: 01392 433546

Frome County Court *(See Trowbridge).*

Gateshead County Court
5th & 6th floor, Chad House,
Tynegate Precinct, Gateshead NE8 3HZ
Tel: 0191 477 2445/2079
Fax: 0191 477 8562

Gloucester Combined Court Centre
Barton House, 121–127 Eastgate Street,
Gloucester GL1 1QL
Tel: 01452 529351
Fax: 01452 386309

Goole County Court
The Customs House, Stanhope Street,
Goole, N. Humberside DN14 5BJ
Tel: 01405 762909
Fax: 01405 767809

Grantham County Court
9 Avenue Road, Grantham,
Lincs NG31 6RB
Tel: 01476 63638
Fax: 01476 70181

Gravesend County Court
26 King Street, Gravesend, Kent
DA12 2DU
Tel: 01474 321771
Fax: 01474 534811

Grays Thurrock County Court
Crown House, Crown Road,
Grays Thurrock, Essex RM17 6JB
Tel: 01375 383927
Fax: 01375 374791

Great Grimsby Combined Court Centre
Town Hall Square, Great Grimsby,
S. Humberside DN31 1HX
Tel: 01472 311811
Fax: 01472 312039

Great Yarmouth County Court
4th Floor, Havenbridge House,
North Quay, Great Yarmouth, Norfolk
NR30 1HZ
Tel: 01493 843132
Fax: 01493 331533

Guilford County Court
The Law Court, Mary Road,
Guildford, Surrey GU1 4PS
Tel: 01483 34991
Fax: 01483 300031

Halifax County Court
Prescott Street, Halifax, W. Yorks
HX1 2JJ
Tel: 01422 552924/355910
Fax: 01422 360132

Hanley County Court *(See Stoke on Trent)*

Harlow County Court
Gate House, The High, Harlow
CM20 1UW
Tel: 01279 443291/2
Fax: 01279 451110

Harrogate County Court
12a North Park Road, Harrogate,
N. Yorks HG1 5PY
Tel: 01423 564837/503921
Fax: 01423 528679

Hartlepool County Court
Law Courts, Victoria Rd, Hartlepool,
Cleveland TS24 8BS
Tel: 01429 268198
Fax: 01429 862550

Hastings County Court
Law Courts, Bohemia Rd, Hastings,
East Sussex TN34 1OX
Tel: 01424 435128
Fax: 01424 421585

Haverfordwest County Court
Crown Buildings, Cherry Grove,
Haverfordwest, Dyfed SA61 2NN
Tel: 01437 765741/2
Fax: 01437 769222

Haywards Heath County Court
Milton House, Milton Rd, Haywards
Heath, West Sussex RH16 1YZ
Tel: 01444 456326
Fax: 01444 415282

Hemel Hempstead County Court
1 Selden Hill, Hemel Hempstead,
Herts HP2 4TX
Tel: 01442 65593
Fax: 01442 219359

Hereford County Court
First Floor, Barclays Bank Chambers,
1/3 Broad Street, Hereford HR4 9BA
Tel: 01432 357233/357571
Fax: 01432 501274

High Wycombe County Court
The Law Courts, Easton Street,
High Wycombe, Bucks HP11 1LR
Tel: 01494 436374
Fax: 01494 459430

Hitchin County Court
Park House, 1–12 Old Park Rd,
Hitchin, Herts SG5 1LX
Tel: 01462 434218/450011
Fax: 01462 432161

Holywell County Court
County Court Buildings,
4 Halkyn Street,Holywell, Clwyd
CH8 7TE
Tel: 01352 711027
Fax: 01352 715024

Horsham County Court
The Law Courts, Hurst Rd,
Horsham, Sussex RH12 2EU
Tel: 01403 252474
Fax: 01403 258844

Huddersfield County Court
Queensgate House, Queensgate,
Huddersfield, W. Yorks HD1 2RR
Tel: 01484 421043/435085
Fax: 01484 426366

Kingston-upon-Hull Combined Courts
Lowgate, Kingston upon Hull, Hull 2EZ
Tel: 01482 568161
Fax: 01482 588527

Huntingdon County Court
Ground Floor, Godwin House,
George Street, Huntingdon, Cambs
PE18 6BD
Tel: 01480 457953
Fax: 01480 435397

Ilford County Court,
Buckingham Rd, Ilford, Essex 1G1 1TP
Tel: 0208 478 1132/3/4
Fax: 0208 553 2824

Ipswich County Court.
8 Arcade Street, Ipswich, Suffolk IPI 1EJ
Tel: 01473 214256
Fax: 01473 251797

Keighley County Court
Yorkshire Bank Chambers, North Street,
Keighley, W. Yorks BD21 3SH
Tel: 01535 602803
Fax: 01535 610549

Kendal County Court
The Court House, Burnside Rd,
Kendal LA9 4NF
Tel: 01539 721218
Fax: 01539 733840

Kettering County Court
Government Buildings, Dryland Street,
Ketering, Northants NN16 0BH
Tel: 01536 512471
Fax: 01536 416857

Kidderminster County Court
Comberton Place, Kidderminster,
Worcs DY10 1QR
Tel: 01562 822480
Fax: 01562 827809

Kings Lyn County Court
Chequer House, 12 King Street,
Kings Lyn, Norfolk PE30 1ES
Tel: 01553 772067/6764597
Fax: 01553 769824

Kingston-upon-Thames County Court
St James Rd, Kingston-upon-Thames
KT1 2AD
Tel: 0208 546 8843
Fax: 0208 547 1426

Lambeth County Court
Court House, Cleaver Street,
Kennington Rd, London SE11 4DZ
Tel: 0207 735 4425/9
Fax: 0207 735 8147

Lancaster County Court
2nd Floor, Mitre House, Church Street,
Lancaster LA1 1UY
Tel: 01524 68112/3
Fax: 01524 846478

Leeds Combined Court Centre
The Courthouse, 1 Oxford Row,
Leeds LS1 3BG
Tel: 0113 283 0040
Fax: 0113 244 8507

Leicester County Court
PO Box 3, 90 Wellington Street,
Leicester LE1 6ZZ
Tel: 0116 265 3400
Fax: 0116 265 3450

Leigh County Court
22 Walmesley Rd, Leigh, Lancs
WN7 1YF
Tel: 01942 673639
Fax: 01942 6811216

Lewes Combined Court
The Law Courts, High Street,
Lewes, E. Sussex BN7 1YB
Tel: 01273 480400
Fax: 01273 476718

Lichfield County Court
Beaconsfield House,Sandford Street,
Lichfield, Staffs WS13 6QA
Tel: 01543 262 137
Fax: 01543 419 443

Lincoln Combined Court Centre
360 High Street, Lincoln LN5 7RL
Tel: 01522 521500
Fax: 01522 511150

Liverpool Combined Court Centre
The Queen Elizabeth 11 Law Courts,
Derby Square, Livererpool L2 1XA
Tel: 0151 473 7373
Fax: 0151 258 1587

Llanelli County Court
2nd Floor, Magistrate's Court Buildings,
Town Hall Square, Llanelli, Dyfed
SA15 3AL
Tel: 01554 757171
Fax: 01554 758079

Llangerfni County Court
County Court Buildings, Glanhwfa
Road, Llangfni, Gwynedd LL77 7EN
Tel: 01248 750225
Fax: 01248 750778

Loughborough County Court
Crown House, Southfield Road,
Loughborough, Leics LE11 2TS
Tel: 01509 267646
Fax: 01509 260096

Lowestoft County Court
Lyndhurst, 28 Gordon Road,
Lowestoft, Suffolk NR32 1NL
Tel: 01502 586047
Fax: 01502 569319

Ludlow County Court
9–10 King Street, Ludlow, Salop
SY8 1QW
Tel: 01584 872091
Fax: 01584 877606

Luton County Court
2nd Floor, Cresta House,
Alma Street, Luton
Tel: 01582 35671
Fax: 01582 24752

Macclesfield County Court
4th Floor, London and Manchester
House, Park Green, Macclesfield
SK11 7QP
Tel: 01625 432492
Fax: 01625 501262

Maidstone Combined Court Centre
The Law Courts, Barker Rd,
Maidstone, Kent ME16 8EQ
Tel: 01622 202000
Fax: CRONN 01622 202001
     CTY 01622 202002

Manchester County Court
Courts of Justice, Crown Square,
Manchester M60 9DJ
Tel: 0161 954 1800
Fax: 0161 839 2756

Mansfield County Court
Clerkson House, St Peters Way,
Mansfield, Notts NG18 1BQ
Tel: 01623 656406
Fax: 01623 26561

Mayor's and City of London Court
32 Threadneedle street, London
EC2R 8AY
Tel: 0207 256 9992
Fax: 0207 256 9991

Medway County Court
Anchorage House, 47/67 High Street,
Chatham, Kent ME4 4DW
Tel: 01634 402881
Fax: 01634 811332

Melton Mowbray County Court
50–52 Scalford Road, Melton Mowbray,
Leics LE13 1JY
Tel: 01664 58336
Fax: 01664 480241

**Merthyr Tydfil Combined Court
Centre**
The Law Courts, Glebeland Place,
Merthyr Tydfil, Mid Glamorfan
CF47 8BH.
Tel: 01685 388307
Fax: 01685 359727

Middlesborough County Court *(See
Teeside CCC)*

Milton Keynes County Court
351 Silbury Boulevard, Central Milton
Keynes MK9 2DT
Tel: 01908 668855
Fax: 01908 230063

Mold County Court
Law Courts, County Civic Centre,
Mold, Clwyd CH7 JAE
Tel: 01352 700313
Fax: 01352 700297

Monmouth County Court
Market Hall, Priory Street,
Monmouth, Gwent NP5 3XA
Tel: 01600 713291
Fax: 01600 712746

Morpeth County Court
17 Market Place, Morpeth,
Northumberland NE61 1LZ
Tel: 01670 512221
Fax: 01670 504188

Neath & Port Talbot County Court
Forster Road, Neath, W. Glamorgan
SA11 3BN
Tel: 01639 642267/8
Fax: 01639 633505

Nelson County Court,
Phoenix Chambers,
9/13 Holme Street, Nelson, Lancs
BB9 0SS
Tel: 01282 601177
Fax: 01282 619557

Newark County Court
The County Court, Crown Building,
41 Lombard Street, Newark, Notts
NG24 1XN
Tel: 01636 703607
Fax: 01636 613726

Newbury County Court
Kings Road West, Newbury,
Berks RG14 5AH
Tel: 01635 40928
Fax: 01635 37704

**Newcastle-upon-Tyne Combined
Courts**
The Law Courts, Quaysisde,
Newcastle-upon-Tyne NE1 3LA
Tel: 0191 201 2000
Fax: 0191 201 2001

Newport (Gwent) County Court
Olympia House, 3rd Floor, Upper Dock
Street, Newport, Gwent NP9 JPQ
Tel: 01633 255267

Newport (I.O.W.) Combined Courts
1 Quay Street, Newport, I.O.W.
PO30 5YT
Tel: 01983 526 821/525 546
Fax: 01983 821 039

**Northampton Combined Court
Centre**
85–87 Lady's Lane, Northampton
NN1 3HQ
Tel: 01604 250 131
Fax: 01604 232 398

North Shields County Court
Northumbria House, Norfolk Street,
North Shields NE30 1EX
Tel: 0191 257 5866
Fax: 0191 296 4268

Northwich County Court
25–27 High Street, Northwich,
Cheshire CW9 5DB
Tel: 01606 42554
Fax: 01606 331490

Norwich Combined Court Centre
The Law Courts, Bishopgate,
Norwich NR3 1UR
Tel: 01603 761776
Fax: 01603 760863

Nottingham Combined Court
60 Canal Street, Nottingham NG1 7EJ
Tel: 0115 979 3500
Fax: 01155 958 7873

Nuneaton County Court
Heron House, Newdegate Street,
Nuneaton, Warwickshire CV11 4EL
Tel: 01203 386 134
Fax: 01203 352 769

Oldham County Court
Church Lane, Oldham, Lancs OLI 3AR
Tel: 0161 620 0425
Fax: 0161 620 0605

Oswestry County Court
2nd Floor, The Guildhall, Bailey Head,
Oswestry, Shropshire SY11 2EW
Tel: 01691 652127
Fax: 01691 71239

Oxford Combined Court Centre
St Aldgates, Oxford OXI ITL
Tel: 01865 264200
Fax: 01865 790773

Penrith County Court
The Court House, Lowther Terrace,
Penrith, Cumbria CA11 7QL
Tel: 01768 862535
Fax: 01768 899700

Penzance County Court
Trevear, Alverton, Penzance,
Cornwall TR18 4JH
Tel: 01736 62987
Fax: 01736 330595

**Peterborough Combined Court
Centre**
Crown Buildings, Rivergate,
Peterborough PEI IEJ
Tel: 01733 349161
Fax: 01733 557348

Plymouth Combined Court Centre
The Law Courts, Armada Way,
Plymouth, Devon PL1
Tel: 01752 674808
Fax: 01752 251657

Pontefract County Court,
Horsefair House, Horsefair, Pontefract,
W. Yorks WF8 IRJ
Tel: 01977 702 357/704 033
Fax: 01977 600 204

Pontypool County Court
Park Road, Riverside, Pontypool, Gwent
NP4 6NZ
Tel: 01495 762 248
Fax: 01495 762 467

Pontypridd County Court
Courthouse Street, Pontypridd,
Mid. Glamorgan CF37 IJR
Tel: 01443 402 471/402 135
Fax: 01443 480 305

Poole County Court
Law Courts, Civic Centre, Park Road,
Poole BH15 2NS
Tel: 01202 741 150
Fax: 01202 747 245

**Portsmouth Combined Court
Centre**
The Courts of Justice, Portsmouth,
Hants POI 2EB
Tel: 01705 822 281
Fax: 01705 826 385

**Preston County Court Combined
Court**
Openshaw Place, Ringway, Preston,
Lancs PRI 2U
Tel: 01772 832 300
Fax: 01772 832 476

Rawtenstall County Court
1 Grange Street Rawtenstall,
Lancs BB4 7RT
Tel: 01706 214 614/212 644
Fax: 01706 219 814

Reading County Court
160–163 Friar Street, Reading RG1 1HE
Tel: 01734 599833
Fax: 01734 391 892

Redditch County Court
13 Church Road, Redditch, Worcs
B97 4AB
Tel: 01527 67822
Fax: 01527 65791

Reigate County Court
Law Courts, Hatchlands Road,
Redhill, Surrey RH1 6BL
Tel: 01737 763637
Fax: 01737 766917

Rhyl County Court
64 Brighton Road, Rhyl, Clwyd
LL18 3HR
Tel: 01745 330216
Fax: 01745 336726

Rochdale County Court
Fleece Street, Rochdale, Lancs
OL16 1ND
Tel: 01706 46862/45377
Fax: 01706 715 576

Romford County Court
2a Oaklands Avenue, Romford,
Essex RM1 4DP
Tel: 01708 750 677
Fax: 01708 756 653

Rotherham County Court
Portland House, Mansfield Road,
Rotherham, S. Yorks S60 2BX
Tel: 01709 364 786/365 544
Fax: 01709 838 044

Royal Courts of Justice
Strand
London WC2
Tel: 0207 936 6000

Rugby County Court
5 Newbold Road, Rugby, CV21 2RN
Tel: 01788 542 543
Fax: 01788 550212

Runcorn County Court
The Law Courts, Shopping City,
Runcorn, Cheshire WA7 2HA
Tel: 01928 716 533
Fax: 01928 701 692

St Albans County Court
Victoria House, Victoria Street,
St Albans AL1 3TJ
Tel: 01727 856 925
Fax: 01727 852 484

St Helens County Court
1st Floor, Rexmore House, Cotham
Street, St Helens, Merseyside WA10 1SE
Tel: 01744 27344
Fax: 01744 20484

Salford County Court
Prince William House, Peel Cross Road,
Salford M5 2RR
Tel: 0161 745 7511
Fax: 0161 745 7202

Salisbury Combined Court Centre,
Alexandra House, St John Street,
Salisbury, Wilts SP1 2PN
Tel: 01722 325 444
Fax: 01722 412 991

Scarborough County Court
9 Northway, Scarborough, N. Yorks
YO11 2EH
Tel: 01723 366361
Fax: 01723 501992

Scunthorpe County Court
Crown Building, Comforts Avenue,
Scunthorpe, S. Humberside DN15 6PR
Tel: 01724 289111
Fax: 01724 291119

**Sheffield County Court
(Combined)**
The Law Courts, 50 West Bar, Sheffield
Tel: 0114 281 2400
Fax: 0114 281 2425

Shoreditch County Court
10 Leonard Street, London EC2A 4AL
Tel: 0207 253 0956
Fax: 0207 490 5613

Shrewsbury County Court
Mardol House, Market Hall Buildings,
Shoplatch, Shrewsbury, Salop SY1 1HS
Tel: 01743 232 650
Fax: 01743 244 479

Skegness and Spilsby County Court
Town Hall Annexe, North Parade,
Skegness PE25 1DA
Tel: 01745 762 429
Fax: 01745 761 165

Skipton County Court
Otley Street, Skipton, N.Yorks BD23 1EH
Tel: 01756 793 315

Slough County Court
The Law Courts, Windsor Road,
Slough, Berks SL1 2HE
Tel: 01753 522 307/8/9
Fax: 01753 575 990

Southampton Combined Court Centre
The Courts of Justice, London Road,
Southampton, Hants SO9 5AF
Tel: 01703 228586
Fax: 01703 220954

Southend County Court
Tylers House, Tylers Avenue,
Southend-on-Sea, Essex SS1 2AW
Tel: 01702 601991
Fax: 01702 603090

Southport County Court
Duke's House, 34 Hoghton Street,
Southport, Merseyside PR9 OPU
Tel: 01704 531 541
Fax: 01704 542 487

South Shields County Court
25/26 Market Place, South Shields,
Tyne & Wear NE33 1AG
Tel: 0191 4563343
Fax: 0191 4279503

Spilsby County Court (*See Skegness & Spilsby*)

Stafford Combined Court
Victoria Square, Stafford ST16 2QQ
Tel: 01785 255217
Fax: 01785 213250

Staines County Court
The Law Courts, Knowle Green,
Staines, Middx TW18 1XH
Tel: 01784 459175
Fax: 01784 460176

Stockport County Court
Heron House, Wellington Street,
Stockport, Cheshire SK1 3DJ
Tel: 0161 4747707
Fax: 0161 4763129

Stoke Combined Court Centre
Bethesda Street, Hanley,
Stoke-on-Trent Staffs ST13BP
Tel: 01782 215076
Fax: 01782 204597

Stourbridge County Court
7 Hagley Road, Stourbridge,
W. Mids DY8 1QL
Tel: 01384 394232
Fax: 01384 441736

Stratford-upon-Avon County Court
5 Elm Court, Arden Street, Stratford-
upon-Avon, Warwickshire CV37 6LW
Tel: 01789 293056
Fax: 01789 293056

Sunderland County Court
44 John Street, Sunderland,
Tyne & Wear SR1 1RB
Tel: 0191 5673691
Fax: 0191 5143028

Swansea County Court
Government Buildings, St Mary's
Square, Swansea, West Glam SA1 3LL
Tel: 01792 472244
Fax: 01792 643444

Swindon Combined Court Centre
The Law Courts, Islington Street,
Swindon SN1 2HG
Tel: 01793 614848
Fax: 01793 618076

Tameside County Court
Scotland Street, Ashton-under-Lyne,
Lancs OL6 6SS
Tel: 0161 3391711
Fax: 0161 3391645

Tamworth County Court
The Precinct, Lower Gungate,
Tamworth, Staffs B79 7AJ
Tel: 01827 62664/55011
Fax: 01827 65289

Taunton Combined Court Centre
The Shire Hall, Taunton,
Somerset TA1 4EU
Tel: 01823 335972
Fax: 01823 322116

Teeside Combined Court Centre
The Law Courts, Russel Street,
Middlesborough, Cleveland TS1 2AE
Tel: 01642 340 000
Fax: 01642 340 002

Telford County Court
Telford Square, Malinsgate, Town
Centre, Telford, Shropshire TF3 4JP
Tel: 01952 291 045
Fax: 01952 291 601

Thanet County Court
Capital House, Northdown Road,
Margate, Kent CT9 1EQ
Tel: 01843 221 722/228 771
        01843 298 997
Fax: 01843 224 313

Torquay County Court
Castle Chambers, Nicholson Road,
Torquay, Devon TQ1 4BS
Tel: 01803 616791
Fax: 01803 616795

Trowbridge County Court
1 Ground Floor, Clarkes Mill,
Stallard Street, Trowbridge BA14 8HD
Tel: 01225 752101
Fax: 01225 776638

Truro Combined Court Centre
The Courts of Justice, Edward Street,
Truro, Cornwall TR1 2PB
Tel: 01872 222340
Fax: 01872 222348

Tunbridge Wells County Court
Merevale House, 42–46 London Road,
Tunbridge Wells, Kent TN1 1DN
Tel: 01892 515515
Fax: 01892 513676

Uxbridge County Court
114 High Street, Uxbridge, Middx
UB8 1DF
Tel: 01895 230441
Fax: 01895 232261

Wakefield County Court
Crown House, 127 Kirkgate, Wakefield,
W. Yorks WF1 1JW
Tel: 01924 370268
Fax: 01924 200818

Walsall County Court
Bridge House, Bridge Street, Walsall,
West Midlands WS1 1JQ
Tel: 01922 432200
Fax: 01922 432212

Wandsworth County Court
76–78 Upper Richmond Road,
Putney, London SW15 2SUR
Tel: 0208 870 2212/6
Fax: 0208 877 9854

**Warrington Combined Court
Centre**
Legh Street, South Warrington,
Cheshire WA1 1UR
Tel: 01295 572192
Fax: 01295 413335

Warwick Combined Court Centre
Northgate South Side, Warwick
CV34 4RB
Tel: 01926 492 276
Fax: 01926 401 266

Watford County Court
Cassiobury House, 11–19 Station Road,
Watford, Herts WD1 1EZ
Tel: 01923 249666
Fax: 01923 251317

Wellingborough County Court
Lothersdale House, West Villa Road,
Wellingborough, Northants NN8 4NF
Tel: 01933 226168
Fax: 01933 272977

Welshpool & Newtown County Court
The Mansion House, 24 Seven Street,
Welshpool SY21 7UX
Tel: 01938 552 004
Fax: 01938 555 395

West Bromwich County Court
2nd Floor, Spencer House,
335/337 High Street, West Bromwich,
W. Mids B70 8RF
Tel: 0121 5005101
Fax: 0121 5800115

West London County Court
43 North End Road, West Kensington,
London W14 8SZ
Tel: 0207 602 8444/6
Fax: 0207 602 1820

Weston Super Mare County Court
2nd Floor, Regent House, 115 High
Street,
Weston Super Mare, Avon BS23 1JF
Tel: 01934 626967/627787

Weymouth & Dorchester Combined Courts
2nd Floor, Westwey House, Westwey
Road, Weymouth, Dorset DT4 8TE
Tel: 01305 778684
Fax: 01305 788293

Whithaven County Court
Old Town Hall, Duke Street,
Whitehaven
Tel: 01946 67788
Fax: 01946 691219

Wigan County Court
Crawford Street, Wigan, Lancs
WN1 1NG
Tel: 01942 246481
Fax: 01942 829164

Willesden County Court
9 Acton Lane, Harlesden,
London NW10 8SB
Tel: 0208 963 8200
Fax: 0208 543 0946

Winchester Combined Court Centre
The Law Courts, The Casele,
Winchester, Hants SO23 9EL
Tel: 01962 841212
Fax: 01962 853821

Wolverhampton Combined Court Centre
Pipers Row, Wolverhampton WV1 3LQ
Tel: 01902 481 000
Fax: 01902 481 001

Woolwich County Court
The Court House, Powis Street, London
SE18 6JW
Tel: 0208 8542127/8948
Fax 0208 3164842

Worcester County Court
The Shire Hall, 48 Foregate Street,
Worcester WR1 1EQ
Tel: 01905 730 800
Fax: 01905 730 801

Workington County Court
Langdale House, Gray Street,
Workington, Cumbria CA14 2PA
Tel: 01900 603967
Fax: 01900 68001

Worksop County Court
8 Slack Walk, Worksop, Notts S80 1LN
Tel: 01909 472358
Fax: 01909 530181

Worthing County Court
The Law Court, Christchurch Road,
Worthing, Sussex BN11 1JD
Tel: 01903 206721
Fax: 01903 235559

Wrexham County Court
2nd Floor, 31 Chester Street,
Wrexham, Clwyd LL13 8XN
Tel: 01978 351738
Fax: 01978 290677

Yeovil County Court
22 Hendford, Yeovil, Somerset
Tel: 01935 74133
Fax: 01935 410004

York County Court
Aldwark House, (off Goodramgate)
York YO1 2BX
Tel: 01904 629935
Fax: 01904 679963

Crown Courts

Aylesbury Crown Court
38 Market Square, Aylesbury,
Bucks HP20 1XD
Tel: 01296 434401
Fax: 01296 435 665

Barnstaple Crown Court
Taunton Combined Court Centre,
Shire Hall, Taunton, Somerset TA1 4EU
Tel: 01823 335972
Fax: 01823 322116

Barrow-in-Furness Crown Court
Sessions House, PO Box 37,
Lancaster Road, Preston PR1 2PD
Tel: 01772 823431

Birmingham Crown Court,
Queen Elizabeth 11 Law Courts,
Newton Street, Birmingham B4 7NA
Tel: 0121 2369751
Fax: 0121 2360606

Bolton Combined Court Centre
Manchester Group Crown Court, The
Law Courts, Blackhorse Street, Bolton,
Lancs BL1 1SU
Tel: 01204 392881
Fax: 01204 363204

**Bournemouth Combined Court
Centre**
Old Building, Law Courts, Stafford
Road, Bournemouth, Dorset BH1 1PN
Tel: 01202 556461
Fax: 01202 290845

Brighton Crown Court *(see Lewes)*

Bristol Crown Court
The Law Courts, Small Street, Bristol
BS1 1DA
Tel: 0117 9763030
Fax: 0117 9763074

Burnley Combined Court Centre
The Law Courts, PO Box 30,
Hammerton Street, Burnley BB11 1XD
Tel: 01282 416899
Fax: 01282 414911

Bury St Edmunds Crown Court
The Court House, Civic Drive, Ipswich,
Suffolk 1P1 2DX
Tel: 01473 213841
Fax: 01473 226606

Caernarfon Crown Court
The Castle, Chester CH1 2AN
Tel: 01244 317606/7/8/9
Fax: 01286 678201

Cambridge Crown Court
The Crown Court, Norwich Union
House, 10 Downing Street, Cambridge
CB2 3DS
Tel: 01223 644367
Fax: 01223 324775

Canterbury Combined Court Centre
Riding Gate House, 37 Old Dover Road,
Canterbury, Kent CT1 3JD
Tel: 01227 462383
Fax: 01227 766752

Cardiff Crown Court
Law Courts, Cathays Park, Cardiff
CF1 3PG
Tel: 01222 345931
Fax: 01222 377865

Carlisle Crown Court
Combined Court Centre, Courts of
Justice, Earl Street, Cumbria CA1 1DJ
Tel: 01228 20619
Fax: 01228 590588

Carmarthen Crown Court
The Law Courts, St Helens Road,
Swansea, W. Glam SA1 4PF
Tel: 01792 452821

Central Criminal Court
Central Criminal Court, Old Bailey,
London EC4M 7EH
Tel: 0207 248 3277
Fax: 0207 248 5735

Chelmsford Crown Court
PO Box 9, New Street, Chelmsford,
Essex CM1 1EL
Tel: 01245 603000
Fax: 01245 603011

Chester Crown Court
The Castle, Chester Cheshire CH1 2AN
Tel: 01244 317606
Fax: 01244 329286

Chichester Combined Court Centre,
Maidstone Group Crown Court, 41/42
Southgate, Chichester, Sussex PO19 1SX
Tel: 01243 786151
Fax: 01243 532252

Coventry Combined Court Centre
140 Much Park Street, Coventry,
W. Mids CV1 2SN
Tel: 01203 536166
Fax: 01203 251083

Croydon Combined Court Centre
Maidstone Group Crown Court, The
Law Courts, Altyre Road, Croydon
CR9 5AB
Tel: 0208 681 2533
Fax: 0208 781 1007

Derby Combined Court Centre
Morledge, Derby DE1 2XE
Tel: 01332 622600
Fax: 01332 622543

Devizes Crown Court
The Law Courts, Islington Street,
Swindon, Wilts SN1 2HG
Tel: 01793 614848

Dolgellau Crown Court
The Castle, Chester Cheshire CH1 2AN
Tel: 01244 317606
Fax: 01341 423307

Doncaster Crown Court
Crown Court at Doncaster, College
Road, Doncaster, S Yorkshire DN1 3HS
Tel: 01302 322211
Fax: 01302 329471

Durham Crown Court
Law Courts, Old Elvet, Durham
DH1 3HW
Tel: 0191 3866714
Fax: 0191 3830605

Exeter Combined Court Centre
The Castle, Exeter, Devon EX4 3PS
Tel: 01392 210655
Fax: 01392 56924

Gloucester Combined Court Centre
Shire Hall, Longsmith Street,
Gloucester GL1 2TG
Tel: 01452 301992/3
Fax: 01452 307636

**Great Grimsby Combined Court
Centre**
Town Hall Square, Grimsby,
S. Humberside DN31 1HX
Tel: 01472 311811
Fax: 01472 312039

Guildford Crown Court
Bedford Road, Guildford, Surrey
GU1 4ST
Tel: 01483 506808
Fax: 01483 579545

Harrow Crown Court
Hailsham Drive, Harrow, Middx
HA1 4TU
Tel: 0208 424 2294
Fax: 0208 424 2209

Haverfordwest Crown Court
The Law Courts, St Helens Road,
Swansea, West Glam SA1 4PF
Tel: 01792 459621

Herford Crown Court
Elgar House, Shrub Hill,
Worcester WR4 9EN
Tele 01905 27006

Hove Crown Court
The Court HouseLandsdowne Road,
Hove, E. Sussex BN3 3BN.
Tel: 01273 773841
Fax: 01273 728356

Inner London Crown Court
Sessions House, Newington Causeway,
London SE1 6AZ
Tel: 0207 234 3100
Fax: 0207 234 3222

Ipswich Crown Court
The Courthouse, Civic Drive,
Ipswich, Suffolk 1P1 2DX
Tel: 01473 213841/2
Fax: 01473 226606

Isleworth Crown Court
36 Ridgeway Road, Isleworth,
Middx TW7 5LP
Tel: 0208 568 8811
Fax: 0208 568 5368

Kenton Bar Crown Court *(see Newcastle-upon-Tyne)*

Kings Lynn Crown Court *(see Norwich combined)*
Court House:
The Court House, College Lane, Kings
Lynn, Norfolk
Tel: 01553 760847
Fax: 01553 772873

Kingston-upon-Hull Combined Courts
Longate, Kingston-upon-Hull HU1 2EZ
Tel: 01482 586161
Fax: 01482 588527

Kingston-upon-Thames Crown Court
Canbury Park Road,
Kingston-upon-Thames, Surrey KT2 6JU
Tel: 0208 549 5241
Fax: 0208 546 3470
Court House:
(1) Canbury Park Road
(2) County Hall, Penrhyn Road
0208 546 1050
(3) Sessions House, 17 Ewell Road,
Surbiton, Surrey 0208 399 6691

Knightsbridge Crown Court
1 Pocock Street, London SE1 OBT
Tel: 0207 922 5800
Fax: 0207 922 5815

Knutsford Crown Court
The Castle, Chester CH1 2AN
Tel: 01244 317606
Court House:
The Sessions House, Knutsford
Tel: 01565 755486
Fax: 01565 652454

Lancaster Crown Court
The Sessions House, PO Box 37,
Lancaster Road, Preston, Lancs PR1 2PD
Tel: 01772 823 431
Fax: 01772 832 300

Leeds Combined Court Centre
The Courthouse, 1 Oxford Row,
Leeds LS1 3BG
Tel: 0113 2830040
Fax: 0113 2448507

Leicester Crown Court
90 Wellington Street, Leicester LE1 6HG
Tel: 0116 265 3400
Fax: 0116 265 3440

Lewes Combined Court
The Law Courts, High Street, Lewes,
East Sussex BN7 1YB
Tel: 01273 480 400
Fax: 01273 476 718
Court House:
(1) The Law Courts, High Street
(2) The Law Courts, Edward Street.
     Brighton 01903 206721
Also sittings at:
(3) **Hove Crown Court**
     The Court House, Lansdowne Road,
     Hove, E Sussex BN3 3BN
     Tel: 01273 773841
     Fax: 01273 728356

Lincoln Combined Court Centre
360 High Street, Lincoln LN5 7RL
Tel: 01522 521500
Fax: 01522 511150

Liverpool Combined Court Centre
The Queen Elizabeth 11 Law Courts,
Derby Square, Liverpool L2 1XA
Tel: 0151 4737373
Fax: 0151 2581587

Luton Crown Court Centre
7 George Street, Luton,
Bedfordshire LU1 2AA
Tel: 01582 488488
Fax: 01582 400450

Maidston Combined Court Centre
The Law Courts, Barker Road,
Maidstone, Kent ME16 8EQ
Tel: 01622 754966
Fax: 01622 687349

Manchester Crown Court
Courts of Justice, Crown Square,
Manchester M3 3FL
Tel: 0161 8328393
Fax: 0161 8325179

Merthyr Tydfil Combined Court Centre
The Law Courts, Glebeland Place,
Merthyr Tydfil, Mid Glamorgan
CF47 8BH
Tel: 01685 388307
Fax: 01685 359727

Middlesborough Crown Court *(See Teeside)*

Middlesex Guildhall Crown Court
Middlesex Guildhall,
Broad Sanctuary, Parliament Square,
Westminster, London SW1P 3BB
Tel: 0207 799 2131
Fax: 0207 233 1612

Mold Crown Court
The Castle, Chester CH1 2AN
Tel: 01244 317606
Court House:
Law Courts, County Civic Centre, Mold,
Clwyd CH7 1AE
Tel: 01352 754343
Fax: 01352 753874

Newcastle-upon-Tyne Combined Courts
The Law Courts, Quayside,
Newcastle-upon-Tyne NE1 3LA
Tel: 0191 201 2000
Fax: 0191 201 2001

Newport (Gwent) Crown Court
Faulkner Road, Newport, Gwent
NP9 4PD
Tel: 01633 266211
Fax: 01633 216824

Newport (I.O.W.) Combined Courts
1 Quay Street, Newport, I.O.W.
PO30 5YT
Tel: 01983 526821

Northampton Combined Court Centre
85/87 Lady's Lane, Northampton
NN1 3HP
Tel: 01604 250131
Fax: 01604 232382

Norwich Combined Court Centre
The Law Courts, Bishopgate,
Norwich NR3 1UR
Tel: 01603 761776
Fax: 01603 760863

Nottingham Combined Court
60 Canal Street, Nottingham NG1 7EJ
Tel: 0115 9793500
Fax: 0115 9590004

Oxford Combined Court Centre
St Aldgates, Oxford OX1 1TL
Tel: 01865 264200
Fax: 01865 790773

Peterborough Combined Court Centre
Crown Buildings, Rivergate,
Peterborough PE1 1EJ
Tel: 01733 534 6342/534 9161
Fax: 01733 557348

Plymouth Combined Court Centre
The Law Courts, Armada Way,
Plymouth, Devon PL1 2ER
Tel: 01752 674808
Fax: 01752 661447

Portsmouth Combined Court Centre
The Courts of Jusrtice, Portsmouth,
Hants PO1 2EB
Tel: 01705 822281
Fax: 01705 826385

Preston Crown Court
The Sessions House, Lancaster Road,
Preston, Lancs PR1 2PD
Tel: 01772 823431

Reading Crown Court
Artillery House, Tilehurst Road,
Reading, Berks RG3 2JL
Tel: 01734 595934
Fax: 01734 573068

St Albans Crown Court
The Court Building, Brickett Road,
St Albans, Herts AL1 3HY
Tel: 01727 834481
Fax: 01727 836263

Salisbury Combined Court Centre
Courts of Justice, Alexandra House, St
John Street, Salisbury, Wilts SP1 2PN
Tel: 01722 325444

Sheffield Crown Court
4th Floor, Belgrave House, Bank Street,
Sheffield S1 1EH
Tele 0114 2737511

Shrewsbury Crown Court
The Shire Hall, Abbey Foregate,
Shrewsbury, Salop SY2 6LU.
Tel: 01743 355775/59365
Fax: 01743 240307

Snaresbrook Crown Court
The Courthouse, 75 Hollybush Hill,
Snaresbrook, London E11 1QW
Tel: 0208 982 5500
Fax: 0208 989 1371

Southampton Combined Court Centre
The Courts of Justice, London Road,
Southampton, Hants SO9 5AF
Tel: 01703 228586

Southend Crown Court
PO Box 9 New Street, Chelmsford,
Essex CM1 1EL
Tel: 01245 358222

Southwark Crown Court
1 English Grounds (off Battlebridge
Lane), Tooley Street, Southwark,
London SE1 2HU
Tel: 0207 522 7200
Fax: 0207 522 7300

Stafford Combined Court Centre
Victoria Square, Stafford ST16 2QQ
Tel: 01785 55217
Fax: 01785 213250

**Stoke-on-Trent Combined Court
Centre**
Bethesda Street, Hanley, Stoke-on-Trent,
Staffs ST1 3BP
Tel: 01782 215076
Fax: 01782 223492

Surbiton Crown Court *(See Kingston-
upon-Thames)*
Court House: The Sessions House,
17 Ewell Road, Surbiton, Surrey

Swansea Crown Court
The Law Courts, St Helens Road,
Swansea, W Glam SA1 4PF
Tel: 01792 459621
Fax: 01792 651724

Swindon Combined Court Centre
The Law Courts, Islington Street Street,
Swindon SN1 2HG
Tel: 01793 614848
Fax 01793 618076

Taunton Combined Court Centre
The Shire Hall, Taunton, Somerset
TA1 4EU
Tel: 01823 335972

Teeside Combined Court
Russell Street, Middlesborough,
Cleveland TS1 2AE
Tel: 01642 340 000
Fax: 01642 340 002

Truro Combined Court Centre
The Courts of Justice, Edward Street,
Truro, Cornwall TR1 2PB
Tel: 01872 222340

**Warrington Combined Court
Centre**
Legh Street, Warrington,
Cheshire WA1 1UR
Tel: 01925 572192
Fax: 01925 413335

Warwick Combined Court Centre
Northgate South Side, Warwick
CV34 4RB
Tel: 01926 495428
Fax: 01926 401266

Watford Crown Court *(See St Albans)*
Court House: 48 Kings Close, Watford
WD1 8UP

Welshpool Crown Court
The Castle, Chester CH1 2AN
Tel: 01244 317606

Willesden Crown Court *(See Harrow)*

**Winchester Combined Court
Centre**
The Law Courts, The Casele,
Winchester, Hants SO23 9EL
Tel: 01962 868141
Fax: 01962 853821

**Wolverhampton Crown Court
Centre**
Pipers Row, Wolverhampton WV1 3LQ
Court House: Pipers Row,
Wolverhampton
Tel: 01902 27774

Woodford Crown Court *(See
Snaresbrook)*

Wood Green Crown Court,
Woodall House, Lordship Lane,
London N22 5LF
Tel: 0208 881 1400
Fax: 0208 881 4802

Woolwich Crown Court
2 Belmarsh Road, London SE28 0EY
Tel: 0208 312 7014
Fax: 0208 312 7078

Worcester Crown Court
2nd Floor, Elgar House, Shrub Hill,
Worcester WR4 9EN
Tel: 01905 27006/7

York Crown Court
The Castle, York YOI 1RY
Tel: 01904 54482/645121/2

Police Stations in the UK

The following numbers are the central non-emergency switchboard numbers as published on force websites at the time of printing.

Avon and Somerset Constabulary
Police Headquarters
Tel: 01275 818181

Bedfordshire Police
Force Headquarters
Tel: 01234 841212

Cambridgeshire Constabulary
Police Headquarters
Tel: 01480 456111

Central Scotland Police
Police Headquarters, Stirling
Tel: 01786 456000

Cheshire Police Force
Cheshire Constabulary Headquarters
Tel: 01244 350000

City of London Police
Wood Street Headquarters
Tel: 020 7601 2222

Cleveland Constabulary
Force headquarters
Tel: 01642 326326

Cumbria Constabulary
Force Headquarters
Tel: 01768 891999

Derbyshire Constabulary
Force Headquarters
Tel: 01773 570100

Devon and Cornwall Constabulary
Middlemoor HQ, Exeter
Tel: 08452 777444

Dorset Police
Dorset Police Headquarters, Dorchester
Tel: 01202 552099

Dumfries and Galloway Constabulary
Police Headquarters, Dumfries
Tel: 01387252112

Durham Constabulary
Police Headquarters
Tel: 0191 386 4929

Dyfed-Powys Police Authority
Police Headquarters, Carmarthen
Tel: 01267 226440

Essex Police
Essex Police Headquarters Chelmsford
Tel: 01245 491491

Fife Constabulary
Police Headquarters
Tel: 01592 418888

Grampian Police
Grampian Police Force Headquarters,
Aberdeen
Tel: 01224 386000

Greater Manchester Police
Force Headquarters
Tel: 0161 8725050

Gwent Police
A Division Headquarters, Newport
   Tel: 01633 244999
B Division Headquarters, Pontytpool
   Tel: 01495 764711
C Division Headquarters, Caerphilly
   Tel: 02920 852999
D Division Headquarters, Cwmbran
   Tel: 01633 838111
E Division Headquarters, Ebbw Vale
   Tel: 01495 350999

Hampshire Constabulary
Central Hampshire Police Divisional
Headquarters, Winchester
Tel: 0845 045 4545

Hertfordshire Constabulary
Hertfordshire Constabulary
Headquarters, Welwyn Garden City
Tel: 01707 354000

Humberside Police Force
Police Headquarters, Hull
Tel: 01482 326111

Kent County Constabulary
Kent County Constabulary Force
Headquarters, Maidstone
Tel: 01622 690690

Lancashire Police Force
Central Switchboard
Tel: 0845 1 25 35 45

Leicestershire Constabulary
Force Headquarters, Leicester
Tel: 0116 222 2222

Lincolnshire Police
Central Switchboard
Tel: 01522 532222

Lothian and Borders Police
Edinburgh
Tel: 0131 311 3131

Merseyside Police
Central Switchboard
Tel: 0151 709 6010

Metropolitan Police
New Scotland Yard
Tel: 020 7230 1212

Norfolk Constabulary
Norfolk Constabulary, Wymondham
Tel: 01953 424242

Northamptonshire Police
Force Headquarters, Northampton
Tel: 01604 700700

Northumbria Police Force
Northumbria Police Headquarters
Tel: 01661 872555

North Wales Police
North Wales Police Headquarters
Tel: 0845 6071002

North Yorkshire Constabulary
Force Headquarters
Tel: 01609 783131

Nottinghamshire Police
Force Headquarters
Tel: 0115 967 0999

Police Service of Northern Ireland
Central Switchboard
Tel: 028 9065 0222

South Wales Police
Police Headquarters, Bridgend
Tel: 01656 655555

South Yorkshire Police
South Yorkshire Police Headquarters
Tel: 0114 2202020

Staffordshire Police
Force Headquarters
Tel: 01785 257717

Strathclyde Police
Glasgow
Tel: 0141 532 2000

Suffolk Constabulary
Force Headquarters
Tel: 01473 613500

Surrey Police
Surrey Police HQ, Guildford
Tel: 0845 125 22 22

Sussex Police
Police Headquarters, Lewes
Tel: 0845 60 70 999

Thames Valley Police
Central Switchboard
Tel: 0845 8505505

Warwickshire Police
Main switchboard
Tel: 01926 415000

West Mercia Police
Main switchboard
Tel: 08457 444 888

West Midlands Police
Central Switchboard
Tel: 0845 113 5000

Wiltshire Police
Force Headquarters, Devizes
Tel: 01380 722341

West Yorkshire Police
Central Switchboard
Tel: 0845 6060606

H.M. Prisons

Prison Establishments in England and Wales

Prison Service HQ Library, London SW1P 4LH (tel 020 7217 5548)
Compiled 30 January 2003–07–10

Privately operated prisons are marked*

HMP ACKLINGTON
MORPETH, Northumberland,
NE65 9XF
Tel: (01670) 760411
Fax: (01670) 761362

HMP ALBANY
NEWPORT, Isle of Wight, PO30 5RS
Tel: (01983) 524055
Fax: (01983) 825827

HMP ALTCOURSE*
Higher Lane, Fazakerley,
LIVERPOOL, L9 7LH
Tel: (0151) 522 2000
Fax: (0151) 522 2121

HMP/YOI ASHFIELD*
Shortwood Road, Pucklechurch
BRISTOL, BS16 9QJ
Tel: (0117) 303 8000
Fax: (0117) 303 8001

HMP ASHFORD*
(Opening June 2004)

HMP ASHWELL
OAKHAM, Rutland, LE15 7LF
Tel: (01572) 774100
Fax: (01572) 774101

HMP/YOI ASKHAM GRANGE
Askham Richard, YORK, YO23 3FT
Tel: (01904) 772000
Fax: (01904) 772001

HMYOI AYLESBURY
Bierton Road, AYLESBURY,
Bucks, HP20 1EH
Tel: (01296) 444000
Fax: (01296) 444001

HMP BEDFORD
St. Loyes Street,
BEDFORD, MK40 1HG
Tel: (01234) 358671
Fax: (01234) 273568

HMP BELMARSH
Western Way, Thamesmead,
LONDON SE28 0EB
Tel: (020) 8331 4400
Fax: (020) 8331 4401

HMP BIRMINGHAM
Winson Green Road,
BIRMINGHAM, B18 4AS
Tel: (0121) 554 3838
Fax: (0121) 554 7990

HMP BLAKENHURST*
Hewell Lane, REDDITCH,
Worcestershire, B97 6QS
Tel: (01527) 543348
Fax: (01527) 546382

HMP BLANTYRE HOUSE
Goudhurst, CRANBROOK,
Kent, TN17 2NH
Tel: (01580) 211367
Fax: (01580) 211060

HMP BLUNDESTON
LOWESTOFT, Suffolk, NR32 5BG
Tel: (01502) 734500
Fax: (01502) 734501

HMYOI BRINSFORD
New Road, Featherstone,
WOLVERHAMPTON, WV10 7PY
Tel: (01902) 791118
Fax: (01902) 790889

HMP BRISTOL
19 Cambridge Road, Horfield,
BRISTOL, BS7 8PS
Tel: (0117) 980 8100
Fax: (0117) 980 8013

HMP BRIXTON
P O Box 369, Jebb Avenue,
LONDON, SW2 5XF
Tel: (020) 8588 6000
Fax: (020) 8588 6283

HMP BROCKHILL
REDDITCH, Worcs, B97 6RD
Tel: (01527) 550314
Fax: (01527) 550169

HMP BUCKLEY HALL
Buckley Farm Lane, ROCHDALE,
Lancs, OL12 9DP
Tel: (01706) 861610
Fax: (01706) 711797

HMP BULLINGDON
P O Box 50, BICESTER, Oxon,
OX25 1WD
Tel: (01869) 353100
Fax: (01869) 353101

HMP/YOI BULLWOOD HALL
High Road, HOCKLEY, Essex, SS5 4TE
Tel: (01702) 562800
Fax: (01702) 562801

HMP CAMP HILL
NEWPORT, Isle of Wight, PO30 5PB
Tel: (01983) 527661
Fax: (01983) 520505

HMP CANTERBURY
46 Longport, CANTERBURY,
Kent, CT1 1PJ
Tel: (01227) 762244
Fax: (01227) 450203

HMP/RC CARDIFF
Knox Road, CARDIFF, CF24 0UG
Tel: (029) 2043 3100
Fax: (029) 2043 3318

HMP/YOI CASTINGTON
MORPETH, Northumberland, NE65 9XG
Tel: (01670) 762100
Fax: (01670) 762101

HMP CHANNINGS WOOD
Denbury, NEWTON ABBOTT,
Devon, TQ12 6DW
Tel: (01803) 812361
Fax: (01803) 812593

HMP/YOI CHELMSFORD
200 Springfield Road, CHELMSFORD,
Essex, CM2 6LQ
Tel: (01245) 268651
Fax: (01245) 493041

HMP COLDINGLEY
Bisley, WOKING, Surrey, GU24 9EX
Tel: (01483) 476721
Fax: (01483) 488586

HMP COOKHAM WOOD
ROCHESTER, Kent, ME1 3LU
Tel: (01634) 814981
Fax: (01634) 828921

HMP DARTMOOR
Princetown, YELVERTON,
Devon, PL20 6RR
Tel: (01822) 892000
Fax: (01822) 892001

HMYOI DEERBOLT
Bowes Road, BARNARD CASTLE,
County Durham, DL12 9BG
Tel: (01833) 637561
Fax: (01833) 631736

HMP/YOI DONCASTER*
Off North Bridge, Marshgate,
DONCASTER, South Yorkshire,
DN5 8UX
Tel: (01302) 760870
Fax: (01302) 760851

HMP DORCHESTER
North Square, DORCHESTER,
Dorset, DT1 1JD
Tel: (01305) 266021
Fax: (01305) 266546

HMP DOVEGATE* (opened July 2001)
Uttoxeter, Staffordshire, ST14 8XR
Tel: (01283) 820000
Fax: (01283) 820066

HMYOI DOVER
The Citadel, Western Heights,
DOVER, Kent, CT17 9DR
Tel: (01304) 203848
Fax: (01304) 215165

HMP DOWNVIEW
Sutton Lane, SUTTON, Surrey, SM2 5PD
Tel: (020) 8770 7500
Fax: (020) 8770 7673

HMP/YOI DRAKE HALL
ECCLESHALL, Staffordshire, ST21 6LQ
Tel: (01785) 858100
Fax: (01785) 858010

HMP DURHAM
Old Elvet, DURHAM, DH1 3HU
Tel: (0191) 332 3400
Fax: (0191) 332 3401

HMP/YOI EAST SUTTON PARK
Sutton Valence, MAIDSTONE,
Kent, ME17 3DF
Tel: (01622) 842711
Fax: (01622) 842636

HMP/YOI EASTWOOD PARK
Falfield, WOTTON-UNDER-EDGE,
Gloucestershire, GL12 8DB
Tel: (01454) 262100
Fax: (01454) 262101

HMP ELMLEY
Church Road, EASTCHURCH,
Sheerness, Kent, ME12 4AY
Tel: (01795) 880808
Fax: (01795) 880118

HMP ERLESTOKE
DEVIZES, Wiltshire, SN10 5TU
Tel: (01380) 813475
Fax: (01380) 818221

HMP EVERTHORPE
BROUGH, East Yorkshire, HU15 1RB
Tel: (01430) 422471
Fax: (01430) 421351

HMP/YOI EXETER
New North Road, EXETER,
Devon, EX4 4EX
Tel: (01392) 278321
Fax: (01392) 496952

HMP FEATHERSTONE
New Road, Wolverhampton,
Staffs, WV10 7PU
Tel: (01902) 703000
Fax: (01902) 703001

HMP/YOI FELTHAM
Bedfont Road, FELTHAM,
Middlesex, TW13 4ND
Tel: (020) 8844 5000
Fax: (020) 8844 5001

HMP FORD
ARUNDEL, West Sussex, BN18 0BX
Tel: (01903) 717261
Fax: (01903) 726060

HMP/YOI FOREST BANK*
Agecroft Road, Pendlebury,
MANCHESTER, M27 8FB
Tel: (0161) 925 7000
Fax: (0161) 925 7001

HMP FOSTON HALL
Foston, DERBY, Derbyshire, DE65 5DN
Tel: (01283) 584300
Fax: (01283) 584301

HMP FRANKLAND
Brasside, DURHAM, DH1 5YD
Tel: (0191) 332 3000
Fax: (0191) 332 3001

HMP FULL SUTTON
Full Sutton, YORK, YO41 1PS
Tel: (01759) 375100
Fax: (01759) 371206

HMP GARTH
Ulnes Walton Lane, Leyland,
PRESTON, Lancashire, PR26 8NE
Tel: (01772) 622722
Fax: (01772) 622276

HMP GARTREE
Gallow Field Road,
MARKET HARBOROUGH,
Leicestershire, LE16 7RP
Tel: (01858) 410234
Fax: (01858) 410808

HMYOI/RC GLEN PARVA
Tigers Road, Wigston,
LEICESTER, LE8 4TN
Tel: (0116) 264 3100
Fax: (0116) 264 3000

HMP/YOI GLOUCESTER
Barrack Square, GLOUCESTER, GL1 2JN
Tel: (01452) 529551
Fax: (01452) 523336

HMP GRENDON/SPRING HILL
HMP Grendon, Grendon Underwood,
AYLESBURY, Bucks, HP18 0TL
Tel: (01296) 770301
Fax: (01296) 770756

HMP/YOI GUYS MARSH
SHAFTESBURY, Dorset, SP7 0AH
Tel: (01747) 853344
Fax: (01747) 855414

IRC HASLAR (Immigration
Removal Centre)
2 Dolphin Way, GOSPORT,
Hampshire, PO12 2AW
Tel: (02392) 580381
Fax: (02392) 510266

HMYOI HATFIELD
Thorne Road, Hatfield, DONCASTER,
South Yorkshire, DN7 6EL
Tel: (01405) 812336
Fax: (01405) 813325

HMP HAVERIGG
MILLOM, Cumbria, LA18 4NA
Tel: (01229) 772131
Fax: (01229) 770011

HMP HEWELL GRANGE
REDDITCH, Worcs, B97 6QQ
Tel: (01527) 550843
Fax: (01527) 550178

HMP HIGH DOWN
Sutton Lane, SUTTON,
Surrey, SM2 5PJ
Tel: (020) 8643 0063
Fax: (020) 8643 2035

HMP/YOI HIGHPOINT
Stradishall, NEWMARKET,
Suffolk, CB8 9YG
Tel: (01440) 823100
Fax: (01440) 823099

HMYOI HINDLEY
Gibson Street, Bickershaw, WIGAN,
Lancashire, WN2 5TH
Tel: (01942) 855000
Fax: (01942) 855001

**HMP HOLLESLEY BAY/HMYOI
WARREN HILL**
WOODBRIDGE, Suffolk, IP12 3JW
Tel: (01394) 411741
Fax: (01394) 411071

HMP/YOI HOLLOWAY
Parkhurst Road, LONDON, N7 0NU
Tel: (020) 7607 6747
Fax: (020) 7700 0269

HMP HOLME HOUSE
Holme House Road,
STOCKTON-ON-TEES,
Cleveland, TS18 2QU
Tel: (01642) 744000
Fax: (01642) 744001

HMP HULL
Hedon Road, HULL, HU9 5LS
Tel: (01482) 282200
Fax: (01482) 282400

HMYOI HUNTERCOMBE
Huntercombe Place, Nuffield,
HENLEY-ON-THAMES,
Oxfordshire, RG9 5SB
Tel: (01491) 641711/6
Fax: (01491) 641902

HMP KINGSTON
122 Milton Road, PORTSMOUTH,
Hampshire, PO3 6AS
Tel: (023) 9289 1100
Fax: (023) 9289 1181

HMP KIRKHAM
Freckleton Road, PRESTON,
Lancashire, PR4 2RN
Tel: (01772) 684343
Fax: (01772) 682855

HMP KIRKLEVINGTON GRANGE
YARM, Cleveland, TS15 9PA
Tel: (01642) 792600
Fax: (01642) 792601

HMP LANCASTER
The Castle, LANCASTER, Lancs,
LA1 1YL
Tel: (01524) 385100
Fax: (01524) 385101

HMP/YOI LANCASTER FARMS
Far Moor Lane, Stone Row Head,
off Quernmore Road, LANCASTER,
LA1 3QZ
Tel: (01524) 848745
Fax: (01524) 849308

HMP LATCHMERE HOUSE
Church Road, Ham Common,
RICHMOND, Surrey, TW10 5HH
Tel: (020) 8948 0215
Fax: (020) 8332 1359

HMP LEEDS
Armley, LEEDS, West Yorkshire,
LS12 2TJ
Tel: (0113) 203 2600
Fax: (0113) 203 2601

HMP LEICESTER
Welford Road, LEICESTER, LE2 7AJ
Tel: (0116) 2546911
Fax: (0116) 2471753

HMP/YOI LEWES
Brighton Road, LEWES,
East Sussex, BN7 1EA
Tel: (01273) 405100
Fax: (01273) 405101

HMP LEYHILL
WOTTON-UNDER-EDGE,
Gloucestershire, GL12 8HL
Tel: (01454) 260681
Fax: (01454) 261702

HMP LINCOLN
Greetwell Road, LINCOLN, LN2 4BD
Tel: (01522) 533633
Fax: (01522) 532116

HMP LINDHOLME
Bawtry Road, Hatfield Woodhouse,
DONCASTER, DN7 6EE
Tel: (01302) 848700
Fax: (01302) 848750

HMP LITTLEHEY
Perry, HUNTINGDON,
Cambridgeshire, PE28 0SR
Tel: (01480) 812202
Fax: (01480) 812151

HMP LIVERPOOL
68 Hornby Road, LIVERPOOL, L9 3DF
Tel: (0151) 530 4000
Fax: (0151) 530 4001

HMP LONG LARTIN
South Littleton, EVESHAM,
Worcestershire, WR11 5TZ
Tel: (01386) 835100
Fax: (01386) 835101

HMP LOWDHAM GRANGE*
LOWDHAM
Nottinghamshire, NG14 7TA
Tel: (0115) 966 9200
Fax: (0115) 966 9220

HMYOI LOW NEWTON
Brasside, DURHAM, DH1 3YA
Tel: (0191) 376 4000
Fax: (0191) 376 4001

HMP MAIDSTONE
36 County Road, MAIDSTONE,
Kent, ME14 1UZ
Tel: (01622) 775300
Fax: (01622) 775301

HMP MANCHESTER
Southall Street, MANCHESTER,
M60 9AH
Tel: (0161) 8175600
Fax: (0161) 8175601

HMP/YOI MOORLAND
Bawtry Road, Hatfield Woodhouse,
DONCASTER, South Yorkshire,
DN7 6BW
Tel: (01302) 351500
Fax: (01302) 350896

HMP MORTON HALL
Swinderby, LINCOLN, LN6 9PT
Tel: (01522) 866700
Fax: (01522) 866750

HMP THE MOUNT
Molyneaux Avenue, Bovingdon,
HEMEL HEMPSTEAD,
Herts, HP3 0NZ
Tel: (01442) 834363
Fax: (01442) 834321

HMP/YOI NEW HALL
Dial Wood, Flockton, WAKEFIELD,
West Yorkshire, WF4 4AX
Tel: (01924) 844200
Fax: (01924) 844201

HMYOI NORTHALLERTON
15A East Road, NORTHALLERTON,
North Yorkshire, DL6 1NW
Tel: (01609) 780078
Fax: (01609) 779664

HMP NORTH SEA CAMP
Freiston, BOSTON,
Lincolnshire, PE22 0QX
Tel: (01205) 769300
Fax: (01205) 769301

HMP/YOI NORWICH
Mousehold, NORWICH,
Norfolk, NR1 4LU
Tel: (01603) 708600
Fax: (01603) 708601

HMP NOTTINGHAM
Perry Road, Sherwood,
NOTTINGHAM, NG5 3AG
Tel: (0115) 962 5022
Fax: (0115) 960 3605

HMYOI ONLEY
Willoughby, RUGBY,
Warwickshire, CV23 8AP
Tel: (01788) 523400
Fax: (01788) 523401

HMP/YOI PARC*
Heol Hopcyn John, BRIDGEND,
Mid-Glamorgan, CF35 6AP
Tel: (01656) 300200
Fax: (01656) 300201

HMP PARKHURST
NEWPORT, Isle of Wight, PO30 5NX
Tel: (01983) 523855
Fax: (01983) 524861

HMP PENTONVILLE
Caledonian Road, LONDON, N7 8TT
Tel: (020) 7607 5353
Fax: (020) 7700 0244

HMP PETERBOROUGH
(opening 2004)

HMYOI PORTLAND
Easton, PORTLAND, Dorset, DT5 1DF
Tel: (01305) 825600
Fax: (01305) 825601

HMP/YOI PRESCOED
Coed-y-Paen, Pontypool,
Gwent, NP14 0TD
Tel: (01291) 672231
Fax: (01291) 672197

HMP PRESTON
2 Ribbleton Lane, PRESTON,
Lancashire, PR1 5AB
Tel: (01772) 257734
Fax: (01772) 556643

HMP RANBY
RETFORD, Nottinghamshire, DN22 8EU
Tel: (01777) 862000
Fax: (01777) 862001

HMYOI & RC READING
Forbury Road, READING, Berks,
RG1 3HY
Tel: (0118) 9587031
Fax: (0118) 9591058

HMP RISLEY
Risley, WARRINGTON,
Cheshire, WA3 6BP
Tel: (01925) 763871
Fax: (01925) 764103

HMP ROCHESTER
1 Fort Road, ROCHESTER,
Kent, ME1 3QS
Tel: (01634) 838100
Fax: (01634) 838101

HMP RYE HILL* (Opened Jan 2001)
Willoughby, RUGBY
Warwickshire, CV23 8AM
Tel: (01788) 523300
Fax: (01788) 523311

HMP SEND
Ripley Road, Send, WOKING,
Surrey, GU23 7LJ
Tel: (01483) 223048
Fax: (01483) 223173

HMP SHEPTON MALLET
Cornhill, SHEPTON MALLET,
Somerset, BA4 5LU
Tel: (01749) 343377
Fax: (01749) 344649

HMP SHREWSBURY
The Dana, SHREWSBURY,
Shropshire, SY1 2HR
Tel: (01743) 352511
Fax: (01743) 356926

HMP SPRING HILL
Grendon Underwood, AYLESBURY,
Bucks, HP18 0TH
Tel: (01296) 770301
Fax: (01296) 770756

HMP STAFFORD
54 Gaol Road, STAFFORD, ST16 3AW
Tel: (01785) 254421
Fax: (01785) 249591

HMP STANDFORD HILL
Church Road, EASTCHURCH,
Sheerness, Kent, ME12 4AA
Tel: (01795) 880441
Fax: (01795) 880267

HMP STOCKEN
Stocken Hall Road, STRETTON,
Nr Oakham, Rutland, LE15 7RD
Tel: (01780) 485100
Fax: (01780) 410767

HMYOI STOKE HEATH
Stoke Heath, MARKET DRAYTON,
Shropshire, TF9 2JL
Tel: (01630) 636000
Fax: (01630) 636001

HMP/YOI STYAL
Styal, WILMSLOW, Cheshire, SK9 4HR
Tel: (01625) 532141
Fax: (01625) 548060

HMP SUDBURY
Ashbourne, DERBYSHIRE, DE6 5HW
Tel: (01283) 584000
Fax: (01283) 584001

HMP SWALESIDE
Barbazon Road, EASTCHURCH,
Sheerness, Kent, ME12 4AX
Tel: (01795) 884100
Fax: (01795) 884200

HMP SWANSEA
200 Oystermouth Road, SWANSEA,
West Glamorgan, SA1 3SR
Tel: (01792) 464030
Fax: (01792) 466127

HMYOI SWINFEN HALL
Swinfen, LICHFIELD, Staffs, WS14 9QS
Tel: (01543) 481229
Fax: (01543) 480138

HMYOI THORN CROSS
Arley Road, Appleton Thorn,
WARRINGTON, Cheshire, WA4 4RL
Tel: (01925) 605100
Fax: (01925) 605101

HMP USK
47 Maryport Street, USK, Gwent,
NP15 1XP
Tel: (01291) 672411
Fax: (01291) 673800

HMP THE VERNE
The Verne, PORTLAND, Dorset,
DT5 1EQ
Tel: (01305) 820124
Fax: (01305) 823724

HMP WAKEFIELD
5 Love Lane, WAKEFIELD,
West Yorkshire, WF2 9AG
Tel: (01924) 378282
Fax: (01924) 299315

HMP WANDSWORTH
PO Box 757, Heathfield Road,
LONDON, SW18 3HS
Tel: (020) 8874 7292
Fax: (020) 8877 0358

HMYOI WARREN HILL
WOODBRIDGE,
Suffolk, IP12 3JW
Tel: (01394) 411741
Fax: (01394) 411071

HMP WAYLAND
Griston, THETFORD, Norfolk, IP25 6RL
Tel: (01953) 858100
Fax: (01953) 858220

HMP WEALSTUN
WETHERBY, West Yorkshire, LS23 7AZ
Tel: (01937) 844844
Fax: (01937) 845862

HMP THE WEARE
Portland Port, PORTLAND,
Dorset, DT5 1PP
Tel: (01305) 822100
Fax: (01305) 820792

HMP WELLINGBOROUGH
Millers Park, Doddington Road,
WELLINGBOROUGH, Northants,
NN8 2NH
Tel: (01933) 224151
Fax: (01933) 273903

HMYOI WERRINGTON
Werrington, STOKE-ON-TRENT,
Staffordshire, ST9 0DX
Tel: (01782) 303514
Fax: (01782) 302504

HMYOI WETHERBY
York Road, WETHERBY,
West Yorkshire, LS22 5ED
Tel: (01937) 585141
Fax: (01937) 586488

HMP WHATTON
14 Cromwell Road, NOTTINGHAM,
NG13 9FQ
Tel: (01949) 850511
Fax: (01949) 850124

HMP WHITEMOOR
Longhill Road, MARCH,
Cambs, PE15 0PR
Tel: (01354) 660653
Fax: (01354) 650783

HMP WINCHESTER
Romsey Road, WINCHESTER,
Hampshire, SO22 5DF
Tel: (01962) 854494
Fax: (01962) 842560

HMP WOLDS*
Everthorpe, BROUGH,
East Yorkshire, HU15 2JZ
Tel: (01430) 421588
Fax: (01430) 421589

HMP WOODHILL
Tattenhoe Street, MILTON KEYNES,
Bucks, MK4 4DA
Tel: (01908) 722000
Fax: (01908) 722001

HMP WORMWOOD SCRUBS
PO Box 757, Du Cane Road,
LONDON, W12 0AE
Tel: (020) 8743 0311
Fax: (020) 8749 5655

HMP WYMOTT
Ulnes Walton Lane, Leyland,
PRESTON, PR26 8LW
Tel: (01772) 421461
Fax: (01772) 455960

Employment Tribunals

Ashford

The Regional Chairman is based in
London South.
Employment Tribunals 1st Floor
Ashford House
County Square Shopping Centre
Ashford
Kent
TN23 1YB
Phone: 01233 621 346
Fax: 01233 624 423
Email: ashfordet@ets.gsi.gov.uk
Download Travel information and map
(PDF format)

Bedford

8–10 Howard Street
Bedford
MK40 3HS
Phone: 01234 351306
Fax: 01234 352315
Email: bedfordet@ets.gsi.gov.uk
Download Travel information and map
(PDF format)

Birmingham

Phoenix House
1–3 Newhall Street
Birmingham
B3 3NH
Phone: 0121 236 6051
Fax: 0121 236 6029
Email: birminghamet@ets.gsi.gov.uk
Download Travel information and map
(PDF format)

Bristol

Ground Floor
The Crescent Centre
Temple Back
Bristol
BS1 6EZ
Phone: 0117 929 8261
Fax: 0117 925 3452
Email: bristolet@ets.gsi.gov.uk
Download Travel information and map
(PDF format)

Bury St. Edmunds

The Regional Chairman is based in
Stratford.
100 Southgate Street
Bury St. Edmunds
IP33 2AQ
Phone: 01284 762171
Fax: 01284 706064
Email: buryet@ets.gsi.gov.uk
Download Travel information and map
(PDF format)
Public Register (Bury St Edmunds)
Visitor Information
Hearing Centre Details – Norwich

Cardiff

Caradog House
1–6 St Andrews Place
Cardiff
CF10 3BE
Phone: 02920 678 100
Fax: 02920 225 906
Email: cardiffet@ets.gsi.gov.uk
Download Travel information and map
(PDF format) (Eng)
Download Travel information and map
(PDF format) (Welsh)

Exeter
The Regional Chairman is based in
Bristol.
2nd Floor
Keble House
Southernhay Gardens
Exeter
EX1 1NT
Phone: 01392 279665
Fax: 01392 430063
Email: exeteret@ets.gsi.gov.uk
Download Travel information and map
(PDF format)
Download Travel information and map
(Faxable PDF format)
Download Travel information and map
(GIF format)

Leeds
3rd Floor
11 Albion Street
Leeds
LS1 5ES
Phone: 0113 245 9741
Fax: 0113 242 8843
Email: leedset@ets.gsi.gov.uk
Travel Information & Map
Hearing Centre Details – Hull

Leicester
The Regional Chairman
is based in Nottingham.
5a New Walk
Leicester
LE1 6TE
Phone: 0116 255 0099
Fax: 0116 255 6099
Email: leicesteret@ets.gsi.gov.uk
Travel Information & Map

Liverpool
The Regional Chairman is based in
Manchester.
1st Floor
Cunard Building
Pier Head
Liverpool
L3 1TS
Phone: 0151 236 9397
Fax: 0151 231 1484
Email: liverpoolet@ets.gsi.gov.uk
Travel Information & Map

London Central
Ground Floor
19–29 Woburn Place
London
WC1H OLU
Phone: 020 7273 8603
Fax: 020 7273 8686
Email: londoncentralet@ets.gsi.gov.uk
Travel Information & Map

London South
Montague Court
101 London Road
West Croydon
CR0 2RF
Phone: 020 8667 9131
Fax: 020 8649 9470
Email: londonsouthet@ets.gsi.gov.uk
Travel Information & Map

Manchester
Alexandra House
14–22 The Parsonage
Manchester
M3 2JA
Phone: 0161 833 0581
Fax: 0161 832 0249
Email: manchesteret@ets.gsi.gov.uk
Travel Information & Map

Newcastle
Quayside House
110 Quayside
Newcastle Upon Tyne
NE1 3DX
Phone: 0191 260 6900
Fax: 0191 222 1680
Email: newcastleet@ets.gsi.gov.uk
Travel Information & Map
Hearing Centre Details – Thornaby
Hearing Centre Details – Carlisle

Nottingham
3rd Floor
Byron House
2a Maid Marian Way
Nottingham NG1 6HS
Phone: 0115 947 5701
Fax: 0115 950 7612
Email: nottinghamet@ets.gsi.gov.uk
Travel Information & Map

Reading
5th Floor
30–31 Friar Street
Reading
RG1 1DY
Phone: 0118 959 4917
Fax: 0118 956 8066
Email: readinget@ets.gsi.gov.uk
Travel Information & Map

Sheffield
The Regional Chairman is based
in Leeds.
14 East Parade
Sheffield
S1 2ET
Phone: 0114 276 0348
Fax: 0114 276 2551
Email: sheffieldet@ets.gsi.gov.uk
Travel Information & Map

Shrewsbury
The Regional Chairman is based
in Cardiff.
Prospect House
Belle Vue Rd
Shrewsbury
SY3 7NR
Phone: 01743 358341
Fax: 01743 244186
Email: shrewsburyet@ets.gsi.gov.uk
Travel Information & Map

Southampton
3rd Floor Duke's Keep
Marsh Lane
Southampton
SO14 3EX
Phone: 023 8071 6400
Fax: 023 8063 5506
Email: southamptonet@ets.gsi.gov.uk
Travel Information & Map
Hearing Centre Details – Brighton

Stratford
44 The Broadway
Stratford
E15 1XH
Phone: 020 8221 0921
Fax: 020 8221 0398
Email: stratfordet@ets.gsi.gov.uk
Travel Information & Map

Watford
The Regional Chairman is based
in Bedford.
3rd Floor
Radius House
51 Clarendon Road
Watford
Hertfordshire WD1 1HU
Phone: 01923 281750
Fax: 01923 281781
Email: watfordet@ets.gsi.gov.uk
Travel Information & Map

INDEX

**For the latest xpl law titles on court procedure,
look at our website www.xplpublishing.com.**

Printed in the United Kingdom
by Lightning Source UK Ltd.
101274UKS00001B/127-168